Refrigerator Rights

Creating Connections and Restoring Relationships

Refrigerator Rights

Creating Connections
and *Restoring Relationships*

Dr. Will Miller
with Dr. Glenn Sparks

A Perigee Book

A Perigee Book
Published by The Berkley Publishing Group
A division of Penguin Putnam Inc.
375 Hudson Street
New York, New York 10014

First edition: November 2002

Visit our website at www.penguinputnam.com

Library of Congress Cataloging-in-Publication Data

Miller, Will, Dr.
    Refrigerator rights : creating connections and restoring relationships / Will
Miller with Glenn Sparks.
        p.   cm.
    ISBN 0-399-52830-X
    1. Interpersonal relations.   2. Social networks.   3. Social isolation.   I. Sparks,
Glenn Grayson.   II. Title.
HM1106 .M547 2002
302—dc21

                                                              2002025280

Printed in the United States of America
10 9 8 7 6 5 4 3 2 1

Contents

Acknowledgments

A book project like this gives one a deep appreciation for the role of a football quarterback, who is often the focus of attention, yet knows how dependent he is on the enormous efforts of those around him. So it is here that I first personally thank Glenn Sparks for his expertise, wisdom, and friendship over the course of several years as he helped me bring to paper the message of *Refrigerator Rights*. His zeal for the project and discipline throughout the endeavor has been an incalculable comfort to me.

Now, on behalf of Glenn and myself we acknowledge the other devoted members of the book's team. Jeff Schwartz and Ian Heller, managers extraordinaire, have been my colleagues and friends for over a decade during my wild and circuitous career ride. They have shared the fun and the heartache, and they are brothers for life. And yes, Linda Roghaar is an outstanding literary agent who guided this project through a four-year roller-coaster ride. But she is a sister to us and kin for life.

We are indebted to Dr. Sally Miller and Dr. Cheri Sparks, the loves of our lives and believers and expert helpers during every step of the process. We want to thank our children and families who freely offered their love and suggestions throughout the process.

We are grateful to Tom Spain, who was the first editor to see the potential for the book's message. His enthusiasm ignited our own passions for the labor. And we are hugely grateful for the expert writing assistance of Molly Wolf, who rescued us when we were awash in words and pages.

And Jennifer Repo, our editor from Penguin Putnam, helped move the project from an exercise in frustration to a labor of love almost overnight. Her enthusiasm for the message and clear guidance about the manuscript altered our experience. We are eternally grateful for her expertise and wisdom. We have been continually bowled over by the enthusiasm of the entire team from Penguin Putnam. It has been a delight to work with everyone there. We are especially grateful to John Duff and Liz Perl and the wonderful people on their staffs, including Beth Mellow and Craig Burke.

We also want to thank all of our refrigerator rights friends—thanks for making us feel like we belong.

How very good and pleasant it is when kindred live together in unity! It is like the precious oil on the head, running down upon the beard, on the beard of Aaron, running down over the collar of his robes. It is like the dew of Hermon, which falls on the mountains of Zion. For there the Lord ordained his blessing, life forevermore.

—PSALM 133

What Are Refrigerator Rights?

Imagine that I come to your home for a first-time visit. We've never met before. We're strangers having a cordial, introductory conversation. You have invited me into your kitchen, and we are sitting together at the table, in the initial stages of getting acquainted. Now, suppose I get up, open your refrigerator, pull out the makings for a sandwich, and start putting them together. Let's face it: Even if you said nothing, you would be surprised and probably affronted. Strangers do *not* open your refrigerator without asking.

But let's change the scene a little. Let's say I'm your brother, come for a visit. While we're catching up on the news, chewing the fat, I get up, open your refrigerator, and grab a cold soda. Are you upset? Of course not. Strangers don't have refrigerator rights, but family members do.

How about this situation: Suppose you and I have been next-door neighbors for three years. During that time we've become good friends. We've celebrated together when good things happened. You invited me to your daughter's graduation party. We've supported each other during times of difficulty. You came to my father's funeral. So when you visited my house on a hot summer day, you asked for a cold drink. "Help yourself," I said, waving at the refrigerator and pointing out where the glasses are. I just granted you refrigerator rights—and so acknowledged that our relationship had turned an important corner. We were more like family. Refrigerator rights refer to the deep, intimate connections that we have with family and the closest friends.

Now for the central question of this book: How many people in your life right now have refrigerator rights in your home? How many of the people you encounter every day see you unshaven or without makeup? How many people hear you express yourself in that blunt, unguarded way you do with your family? How many can you talk to at a real deep, intimate level? And how many people grant *you* refrigerator rights? How many people confide in you— tell you about the things that really matter to them?

It's our belief that modern life has been profoundly affected by the loss of refrigerator rights relationships. We've lost them through three major social changes: *increased mobility, heavy social emphasis on individualism,* and *emotionally numbing distractions.* This book aims to show the connection between our loss of intimacy with people in our lives and the stress and disconnection that we feel in everyday life. This book is for all people who sense a gap between their level of personal and career achievement and their sense of inner peace and contentment. If you feel discontented or dissatisfied, even as you acknowledge that your life is rich and blessed, this may be your story.

The voice of the book is mine, and I will be telling the stories. But I wrote it with my friend and colleague Dr. Glenn Sparks, with whom I have been working for several years. He's a professor of mass communication at Purdue University and a recognized expert on the media and their effects. Glenn has scoured the relevant re- search across several disciplines, including psychology, sociology, and medicine, as well as the demographic data of the U.S. Census Bureau.

For my part, I've spoken about the refrigerator rights concept to corporations and organizations across the country for the past nine years and on radio shows I do each week. In all these venues I have invited listeners to write and share their experiences. I also have promoted the idea and sought feedback from people on my website, www.drwill.com, visited by about 100,000 people each year. I have received a multitude of responses from people who have heard about refrigerator rights in the media or at conferences and have generously shared their personal stories of moving away and losing relationships. Many of their stories are shared in the pages that follow.

But the concept of refrigerator rights goes further and deeper than Glenn's research and the feedback I've received. While we're both well qualified to do an analysis of modern life, this project is deeply rooted in our personal experience. So this is a personal story as well as an intellectual enterprise. And in the age of terror angst, we are reminded that the primal human reaction to a catastrophe that rocks us is to reach out for connection to others for coping and comfort. Our first help is found with another. But this need for deep connection to others is every bit as necessary in our "normal" day-to-day routine as it is in the midst of trauma. The terrorist era has served to help us better understand our fundamental need for connection—a need that had been all but lost in the lunacy of the modern lifestyle.

For the new millennium, we hope to suggest a better compromise between pursuing your life's ambitions and maintaining your emotional well-being. This means creating a lifestyle that cultivates refrigerator rights, deepens intimacy, and restores emotional closeness to your relationships with the people around you. We don't promise that it will be easy. The sad truth is that once the immediate impact of trauma fades in conscious memory, defenses reemerge and old habits of emotional distance resume. How many of us are living our "old normal"? Nonetheless, we are convinced that the restoration of refrigerator rights relationships is essential for life balance. We won't promise that you'll find instant success by following a step-by-step plan. Habits are very difficult to change, and close relationships are very difficult to cultivate. But we believe you *can* restore the lost relationships you need to be happy and at peace. Simply understanding the problem is at least half of the solution.

So that's where we'll start: How on earth did we get ourselves into this condition? In Part One we will talk about what we have done to ourselves and with our freedom. In Part Two, we will offer an overview of how we got into our current circumstances, starting with an examination of mobility and what it does to us. We follow this with an assessment of our professional striving and its effects on our lives. We go on to explore how our use of the media (television, radio, and the Internet) helps to isolate us and impedes our ability to form new attachments. Part Three will outline what we need to flourish as individuals and as a culture, and we close with a perspective on recovering old—or reestablishing new—refrigerator rights relationships.

Before moving on, however, you need to be aware that this book is intended to help you recognize the problem rather than offering any quick-fix solution. The loss of our close relationships is a widespread, systematic problem in the culture. But solutions to the problem are invariably personal and anecdotal. Your reasons for separating from important past relationships are unique to you. You must solve your own dilemma. However, we sincerely believe that you will have the same experience as we have had. The more you see your life's challenges through the lens of losing refrigerator rights, the clearer your path will be toward a life-changing solution.

We have to start where we are: with an overview of modern life as the way many of us are living it. We are a culture of great wealth and opportunity, but also a society of emotional deprivation and surpassing stress. Perhaps you will find a picture of yourself in the next chapter.

Refrigerator Rights

Creating Connections and Restoring Relationships

Part One

How We Live

Losing Refrigerator Rights

And I don't know a soul who's not been battered;
I don't have a friend who feels at ease.

—PAUL SIMON, *"American Tune"*

It's Not Just Me

We all want the same thing: a happy, well-adjusted life with not too many downs and a few really high spots. We want to be at peace with ourselves while at the same time being productive in our careers and close to our nearest and dearest. I'm certainly like this, and so (I suspect) are you. I'm reasonably successful, personally and professionally. But I am bugged by a nagging sensation that I ought to feel better than I do, given how well my life has gone. I should be serene and contented, or so I think. But for the life of me, I've never been able to hang on to serenity for more than an hour at a stretch, or so it seems.

For a long time I assumed it was my biology—that I was hard-wired to be incapable of calm. Certainly I'm an intense individual, but I don't want to exaggerate: I'm social and engaging, and I genuinely want to be a good person. But I often have to battle tendencies that move me in the opposite direction. My intensity is actually anxiety, and I constantly live with its discomforts. It's not that I've got an awful lot to be genuinely anxious about; I'm well aware that my feelings about my life do not match the actual quality of my life. I rarely become melancholy, but I'm frequently too wound up with worry.

Over the years I've tried most of the available remedies. I not only attended psychotherapy, I thoroughly engaged the process. In fact, I became a psychotherapist myself. I've read a great deal of the literature about how to live a full, balanced, and peaceful life, from the abstruse classic masters through the cheesy self-help junk. I've listened attentively to motivational speakers and sat through infomercials about marriage and my inner child. I've explored spirituality, embraced my faith, and even became an ordained minister. I've spent years in the garage of my own mind, tinkering and rebuilding, trying to fix myself. And I've taken myself into the shop for the professionals to have a go. The results are mixed. I have insight and understanding and a capacity to expound on the human condition. But in all honesty, I still have the anxiety.

Was it my family background? I thought it might be—hence all that psychotherapy—but now, from the vantage point of fifty years of experience and perspective, I can see that we were merely ordinarily neurotic, nothing extreme. In the long run I came to realize that, compared to so many others, my psychological problems were trivial. Of course I had issues to address, but in the end I came to recognize that my parents and siblings were healthy and well adjusted enough and did not owe me any more than what they gave, which was plenty. But it took years for me to discover and accept this conclusion. In the meantime, I'd wasted enormous amounts of time and energy exploring my own navel and hopping from one career to another in search of satisfaction. I never gave much thought to whether my angst was normal or common. Instead, I focused only on trying to feel better and fix myself.

Although I still read, reflect, and pray, I am no longer persuaded that my ongoing anxiety and stress symptoms are caused principally by either genetics or childhood experiences. What then? At eighteen I charged out into the world on my own without a second thought about leaving all these people behind. It never occurred to me that I would suffer consequences by disconnecting from my family. I just left . . . and went on leaving. Ever since I went off to college, I've been a moving fool. When I actually calculated the number of times I've relocated since then, I shocked myself. Since graduating from college, I've lived in seventeen different places in six states. I've moved every two years as an adult. Oh, the boxes! Oh, the duct tape! I've lost more personal items than I've kept, and I have stuff in my attic that I packed two moves ago. Images of past apartments and houses float through my mind. My life has been like that of someone fleeing the authorities.

Curiously, late in life, my parents began their own itinerant lifestyle. They've lived in a dozen places in three states, moving constantly to be close to one or more of their seven children who live in seven different states. I am beginning to wonder if we moved simply because we could. But I wonder more what influenced us to become so mobile and disregard the model of stability that characterized our upbringing. I never reflected at all on the loss of contact with my family or the consequences of my choices. Because I have moved so often and my family is so scattered, that stability is now long gone for me. I no longer share my daily life with any of these people I knew and loved. I live wholly apart from the associations of my childhood. For me as for many others, home's not there to go to anymore.

So I now ascribe more of my restless feelings to this loss of my social network—the loss of my "refrigerator rights" relationships (as described in "What Are Refrigerator Rights?" on pp. xi). But it's even more than that. I've come to believe that what I've been feeling for most of my life is the norm for millions of otherwise fully functional, successful individuals—perhaps you? While the symptoms of this malaise vary from one person to another, no one disposition or character type is exempt. For me, it's anxiety. For you, maybe it's a mild sense of depression if not Real Big Depression. If you've tried to describe this mild depression you might say you're just a bit . . . well, discontented. But that really isn't it. Down isn't really it either. You're just not as happy as you know you could be. You've got a nagging sense of melancholy that doesn't go away. You don't have an illness; you're just ill at ease too much of the time.

Some of us have a temperament that predisposes us to discomfort in various ways. I have come to the conclusion, however, that modern life has gnawed away at the cushion that our past refrigerator rights relationships used to provide for our idiosyncratic temperaments. My wife, Sally, has always been easygoing and upbeat, while I'm more torqued-up and tightly wound. Not surprisingly, we manifest our discomforts differently. When I'm anxious or stressed out, I become hyper, impatient, and testy. I have a temper and a sharp tongue and tend to take it out on the people close around me. Sally ruminates over her problems and directs her anger inward. As a result, she endures stomach and digestive problems. She can look peaceful on the outside while she's quietly burning a hole in her gut.

The bottom line is that despite our varying temperaments, we are more uncomfortable than we care to admit . . . or think we should be. Most people we talked to in researching this book identify with our sentiments. Listen to Pam's story:

> I was driving to work this morning and heard you on the radio talking about "refrigerator rights," and I was vigorously nodding my head at what you were saying. I haven't lived near my hometown since 1980. I have relocated twice, the first time to California

and the second time to Iowa, where I've been now for 11 years. I am quite aware that having no extended family near me has had an impact. I'm raising four boys without the support and companionship of family. Friendships have come and gone. My spouse is my only constant companion, and I know that relying on him for everything is not realistic.

I do have two close friends that have "refrigerator rights," but still, I wonder if I have those rights in their homes. This has caused a lot of anguish over the years. In California, I didn't realize what was causing the loneliness. In Iowa, I know—but what does one do about it? The kind of "knowing" someone that comes with blood relation can never fully be realized through a friendship. That takes years, and commitment on both sides.

My husband is in sales and is gone about a third of the year. I have been trying to cultivate friendships that can fill that void, but it isn't easy. Maybe it's my imagination, but it seems like the people around me have their own busy family life and don't need that kind of closeness. It's especially hard during holidays, when friends are with their families and my husband isn't home.

It's Not Just Us

Maybe chronic low-grade discomfort is a condition unique to my generation or, more narrowly, to my socioeconomic peers. Maybe we're just cranky, selfish, college-educated baby boomers. Although my father has never said it out loud, I often suspect that he and his friends believe this. And how can I tell them otherwise? They grew up through the Great Depression and then went straight out of high school and into a harrowing World War. Compared to us they suffered and they sacrificed—not just occasionally, but as a norm for daily living. Who can blame them for looking down their nose at their coddled, self-centered kids? It's no wonder they were suspicious of our motives when we balked at going to Vietnam for a national cause. Our tributes to them as the "Greatest Generation" are well warranted, but perhaps we feel some guilt about our own spotty record of public service.

Whatever the tension between the "Greatest" and the rest of us, it's been an opinion expressed by many that we are the defective generation—that we are stressed out because we are so self-absorbed. I've been inclined to accept this assessment. Now, of course, this has all changed. The terrorist assault on America awakened all of us to the stress of uncertainty. We now have experience that joins us to our forebears and helps us comprehend a bit more fully the emptiness and ultimate futility of a lifestyle of career pursuit and material accumulation.

But this awakening is recent and after the fact. Like so many millions, I grew up in a culture that allowed me the freedom to be ambitious and to plan for the future. I have always had ambitions. Like any kid, I "knew" what I wanted to be when I grew up. It's just that the vision kept changing with each exposure to different possibilities. Everything seemed so possible that nothing really became probable. I went to college with absolutely no vision or plan for my future career or personal life. Sadly, four years later, I graduated without any more clarity. And this was quite common. Many of my peers seemed restless and even aimless. With the exception of a handful of young people in hot pursuit of a career in medicine, law, or business, most of my liberal arts friends had no clue about where we were headed in life. We weren't reflective about our past or worried about our future, except for the draft. We lived utterly in the moment—but not in some highly evolved Zen sense. Quite the opposite: I was always focused on whatever was in front of my nose, like a distracted dog.

For a while it appeared to me that our children's generation had more focus about their life direction. They seem to be more aware that it was up to them to direct their futures. Now, of course, I know better. Glenn, who teaches undergraduate students, observes that, while different from their baby boom parents in many ways, today's young adults are just as stressed as anyone else. When we interview them, many feel unsettled, pressured, and fretful about their lives and future. My own grown stepchildren and their peers seem just as temperamental and goosey as we do. And when I watch my grandsons, riveted to Game Boy, Disney, Nintendo, and television, I can't see really big changes to come. Perhaps the culture has been changed irrevocably by the threat of terrorism and war, but for us it remains to be seen. What we do know is this: The habits of moving and isolation that we have cultivated over the past half century are so embedded that they will not change quickly.

Almost everyone seems to be feeling impatient and often jittery. Even my tranquil, elderly in-laws sense that there is something about the feel of modern existence that isn't quite right. Life is in high gear and speeding by, and it's getting harder to focus. A few years ago I went to see the Indianapolis 500 auto race. From my seat in the stands, the cars were a blur, whipping by at more than 200 miles per hour. I could see the whole pack of cars but couldn't pick out any car in particular. That's how I feel sometimes. I have a larger sense of where we are, but I can't stay focused on any one thing for very long. The result: Life seems off-kilter in some profound way. People I encounter, even the energetic and optimistic, are wrestling with problems of peace and fulfillment.

It's the Stress, Stupid

Most often I hear this current condition described under the umbrella term *stress*. Now, I make my living speaking about stress, so, presumably, I know all about it. I have a confession to make: For a long time, I've been just as uncertain as my audiences about what actually underlies our sense that "something's wrong." I tend to lapse occasionally into the thinking that stress is equivalent to "worry." Most of us tend to think of it that way. If you describe yourself as "stressed out" about something, you probably are referring to the fact that you've been worrying about the consequences of something that did happen or something that might happen.

It's true that worrying is stressful. But few of us really seem to fully appreciate that stress is more than just psychological pressure. It wreaks havoc on the entire physical body. Think about the life pressures that make it harder for your body to function smoothly. In the medical community, anything that makes it difficult for your bodily systems to operate is referred to as a "stressor." If your heart muscle is weak, it stresses the rest of your body. If your back gets wrenched by a fall, your body is stressed. If you lose sleep worrying about money or your rebellious teenage daughter, your body is stressed.

And the particular variable that makes it most difficult for your body to operate properly is change. Any significant change in your life puts additional stress on you. And here's the amazing part: It doesn't matter whether the change is good or bad—it still counts as stressful. Changing jobs, getting married, or reconciling an important relationship are all highly stressful, even though they are positive changes. So with the pace of modern society moving at faster-than-lightning speed, change is the order of the day. We often don't account for the stress these changes put on our whole body, physically and psychologically.

While change may be stressful, our social support system is supposed to shield us from a lot of the impact. Yet many of us are living lives of almost constant change, which has had the effect of diminishing our social network. This strips us of valuable armor in the battle against stress taking its toll on our body. The survivors escaping the disaster at the New York City World Trade Center attack were following deep human instincts when they made urgent, spontaneous connections to complete strangers in the midst of the trauma. While a terrorist attack may serve to highlight the importance of forging connections with others, when the shock wears off, most of us find ourselves back in our same routine. Maybe you are someone who has "stayed put," but have people in your life that are simply passing through. As long as you remain emotionally distant from others, the very insulation you need against stress—close relationships—is diminished. Social and emotional isolation places you at a profound disadvantage when trying to control your stress. And isolation is the ongoing story—perhaps the headline—of the modern age.

I've slowly come to the conclusion that the core emotional problem of modern life is this: *a pervasive personal detachment and aloofness from other people.* And this characterizes life for too many of us. We no longer live in physical or emotional closeness to the people who helped shape us, including our family of origin, friends, neighbors, and the acquaintances of our childhood. And we have failed to replace our social network with new people. It's not just about moving away. It's about being away, being apart, being isolated, and being too alone. It is about the loss of refrigerator rights with others.

When Glenn teaches his students about the impact of mass media on their lives, he often uses the metaphor of fish not noticing the water that makes up their environment. If something is nearly constant or routine, we tend not to notice it. Breathing is so automatic that you don't tend to consciously think about the mechanics of your body as you take a breath. In today's environment, our isolation from other people has become so routine that many of us don't even realize that this is our state of affairs. We may tend to notice our stress a little more because there is more of an ebb and flow to daily anxiety and tension, but rarely do we tend to think about our levels of stress and our isolation from others as essentially interconnected and part of the same problem.

My wife, Sally, was widowed at twenty-four and left with two small children. Talk about change! Looking back, she marvels at her decision in the aftermath to move away from her hometown, family, and friends in order to feel better. "After he died, I didn't want to be around any reminders of Bob. So I wanted to get as far away as I could." Today she is a writer and speaker about grief and loss and attests to change and loss of support as central variables in the stress of grief. "I did exactly the wrong thing," she says. "I needed to be around my family and friends and the familiarity of my home. Instead, I followed my feelings, which were curdled with sadness, anger, and loneliness, and made another life change that was just as devastating."

Life Apart

Each of us has a story that brings to life the loss of refrigerator rights. Mine is not unusual. I come from an apparently functional family, raised by my full-time, stay-at-home mother and a hardworking, blue-collar father. I was born in Brooklyn, New York, in 1949. We lived in a small apartment that soon ran out of room. Fulfilling the dream common to young city families after the war, we moved to Plainview, a New York suburb.

Over those next few years most of my extended family migrated out of Brooklyn to various towns on Long Island as well. Before long, we were all relocated and living within a half-hour's drive of each other. Growing up, my life was filled with an abundance of relationships. I had my big family, the kids at school, and my neighborhood friends. Inside our little ranch house, my parents and the seven kids jostled around, negotiating as much personal independence as we could in close quarters. We had one bathroom, which nine people had to share each morning as we got ready for school or work. As a result, I can now shower and dress for work in less than five minutes. During Army basic training years later, it took me several weeks to realize that the reason I was adapting so well to barracks life was that compared to the tough, *move-move-move* rhythm of my home, the army was a breeze.

Most Sundays my family traded visits and ate dinner with my mother's parents, her two sisters, her brother, and their families. Virtually every week I spent an afternoon with all my aunts, uncles, and first cousins—about twenty-five of us in all. These relationships, while not quite as involved, were every bit as important to me as those in my immediate family. For us, the distinction between nuclear and extended family was a soft line, and we crossed it weekly. Today we live differently, don't we? I know I do. I suspect that you do, too. There is a much sharper divide between nuclear and extended family. And I'm betting—just like me—that the number of people in your life who have refrigerator rights relationships with you has diminished over the years.

Missing Links

You can't really know people from a distance. Reunions don't cut it. My extended family tries to get together at least once each year at a summer picnic or a holiday gathering. But what can I expect to happen in a few hours' time? There is a quick exchange about family events, but it's little more than headline news. I may know that my cousin got a new job, but it's unlikely she will take the time over a hot dog to relate how a recent cancer scare changed her entire outlook on life. If I lived nearby and shared some of her daily life, I would know and be able to offer my care and my prayers. But because she lives so far away, I'm not likely to be up-to-date on the meaningful events in her life. This is so terribly sad. And it's no way to live. But why are so many of us doing this?

What I'm experiencing is not just a matter of physical distance; my own psychological orientation is part of the picture as well. The transition was subtle, but since growing up and moving away, I have developed an altered sense of my family as an adult. As a child, when I thought about "my family" it meant everyone, including my uncles, aunts, and cousins. But now that soft boundary between nuclear and extended family has been hardened, and my sense of family today is limited to my parents, brothers, and sisters. I suppose it's mostly economy of time, but my efforts to stay in touch with my family have been narrowed. And I can barely keep up with my siblings. I simply don't find the time to stay connected to the rest of my kin. E-mail has helped a little, but this is limited and superficial.

There is even a second layer of loss. When we have reunions or periodic visits I hardly know anything about the children of my cousins. They are kin in name, and we know a little about each other, but we don't really know each other the way I desire to know my family. I've lost some relatives to death—my grandparents, my aunt Carol, my cousin Kevin, my uncle Jack. But more subtly, I have lost meaningful connection with many of those others who were so much a part of the relational world that helped shape me.

I guess I thoroughly embraced the freedoms available to me, but now when I look back over my life, I am appalled by the cavalier choices I made. I lost so many of the important attachments and relationships that (I now believe) are needed for a satisfying and less-stressful life. I set out blindly to make my way in the world, narrowly focused on my individual happiness and fulfillment. What I failed to calculate is the cost of my fierce individuality: the loss of emotional resources that turned out to be critical for enjoying my achievements and successes.

What is distressing is that so many can tell the same sort of story. I know a therapist who loves to get together with his old college friends. When we were talking about the loss of refrigerator rights, he noted a connection between the idea and his own longing for college days. He told me about another acquaintance that virtually lives for their reunions and his longing for friends:

> I have always been an active member of my alumni association. For twenty years I've never missed our class get-togethers and re-unions. I have to admit that I have an unflagging enthusiasm for remembering my college days. I had a great group of friends and we became like brothers to each other. I still keep in touch with several of these guys and, no matter how long the gap since we've spoken, we reconnect in an instant. It's great.
>
> But if truth be told, it makes me sad that I have never been able to replicate that experience in my adult life. For a long time I assumed that this was something I could only experience as a young person. Now I'm not really sure. There was no magic to why we became so close. We lived together, studied and ate together, and shared each other's lives as if we were members of the same family. Today, most of my family lives far away. Obviously, my own wife and kids are close, but that's about it. I have no other men in my life that even remotely feel like brothers to me. It seems to me that if the only time you get to enjoy these feelings of being close and connected is at a college or army reunion, something is wrong.

Glenn's personal history also reflects dislocation and separation from family, but in his case, the model for uprooting came early. When he was eleven years old, his parents bought a donut franchise, and they moved from Baltimore, Maryland, to New Jersey. They had dreams of independence and prosperity for the family. Glenn remembers losing contact with his extended family and his neighborhood and the challenge of trying to fit into a new town and school. At the end of that first school year, his parents decided that they needed to be closer to their business, and they moved again to a nearby town. This time, it was to an apartment complex, and the transition was more difficult. Glenn was in junior high, where the social cliques are more resistant to newcomers. After two years, they moved once again to a new location in the same town. Two years later they moved a fourth time to a single-family home, still in the same community. Glenn was in a perpetual state of social adjustment, constantly trying to fit in and find acceptance. He graduated from high school and left the state and his parents for good. Since then, his pattern of moving has continued into his adult years.

He's moved four times since college, three times to different states. At last he settled down and has stayed in one place for sixteen years. But during that time, his oldest son, David, has gone away to college, graduated, and not returned to the homestead. In fact, he left the country. He now lives in South Korea, where he teaches English to Korean children. He tells Glenn he doesn't know when he'll return to the United States. His oldest daughter, Erin, left home to attend the University of Chicago, and Jordan, the youngest, is preparing for her college entrance exams. In just a short span of time, all of his children will probably be away from home, leading their own lives. Today, Glenn and his wife, Cheri, have semi-regular phone and visiting contact with their immediate families, but like me, they have essentially lost their connections with extended family and other long-term relationships.

Even when family members have lived relatively close, there remains a profound sense of being apart. The feel of separation from others appears to be the stamp of modern culture. Some blame it on "the pace of life" and moan about how busy everybody seems to be. Others pontificate about the breakdown of the family as the result of our moral collapse. Some focus attention on the evils of the mass media. The list of culprits is nearly endless.

But Glenn and I don't believe that the difference between the quality of life two generations ago and today is a consequence of either character deterioration or scientific progress. Rather, our strong suspicion is that it's rooted in the now-accepted custom of living the unattached life, moving away, and being apart from those we love, with its unavoidable disturbance of all our relationships.

If you want to test our hypothesis, we suggest you examine your own life. As you read through the rest of this book and contemplate our stories and the stories of others, I encourage you to focus on your own life situation and assess the impact the loss of refrigerator rights has had on you. Who were you close to in your childhood? Your adolescence? Your young adulthood? What has become of those people? Are they gone? Are they still in your life? And perhaps more important, have they been replaced?

Points to Remember

- Many of us feel much more uncomfortable in our day-to-day lives than we care to admit—and more uncomfortable than we think we should be, even allowing for our personal weaknesses that we know so well.

- The core emotional problem of modern life is this: *a pervasive personal detachment and aloofness from other people.*

- Our modern life has been profoundly affected by the loss of "refrigerator rights" relationships—the type of relationships that resemble family interactions—the type of relationships that are so comfortable that you can go into each other's refrigerator with no questions asked.

Life in the Isolation Culture

I never saw a moor, I never saw the sea;
Yet know I how the heather looks, and what a wave must be.
I never spoke with God, nor visited in heaven;
Yet certain am I of the spot as if the chart were given.

—EMILY DICKINSON, "I Never Saw a Moor"

Connecting the Dots

Perhaps you read the first chapter about the loss of refrigerator rights relationships and didn't identify with the predicament. Oh, you could accept that there's a social trend toward separation, but you do not consciously experience it as a problem in your daily life. Perhaps you've lost contact with your family of origin and feel okay. Or you choose not to be close to your family. Or you have a lot of friends. It's just the way things are. You may also feel some degree of life stress, but you don't see any real connection with being apart from family or having very few intimate friends. They're like two dots on a piece of paper with no connection between them.

This chapter connects the dots between isolation and its effects. It describes some of the symptoms that characterize isolated people, and it ties common lifestyle problems to social disconnection. When you're reading it, reflect on your own circumstances. Is isolation a problem for you? We can't tell from here. Maybe you really do have a life full of warm, rewarding human bonds—a whole kitchen full of people with refrigerator rights. Or maybe your kitchen is a place of loneliness and you've just gotten used to the emptiness; you take it for granted. It's just the water you're swimming in right now. Maybe you also feel stressed and a nagging sense of dissatisfaction. If such is the case, maybe *you* need to connect the dots—to make the connection between your isolation and your state of mind.

Below is an exercise we devised called "This Is Your Life." We think it might help you get a feel for your own relationship situation. You may be tempted to glance through the items and think that because many of the symptoms don't particularly seem to fit you, you're not really isolated. But please take your time and answer all the questions. Isolation manifests itself in many different ways. You may fail to see yourself in all or most of the symptoms we describe, but one or two might fit you perfectly. Or perhaps none fit you perfectly, but you may find shades of truth in several.

This Is Your Life

Instructions: Take a few minutes to think about the items below. This brief exercise is designed to help you take stock of your lifestyle. It isn't meant to pigeonhole you into a narrow category, but rather to encourage you to think about yourself and your lifestyle. For each of the statements, think about the extent to which you AGREE or DISAGREE that the statement accurately describes you.

1. As an adult I feel like I have moved my home too many times. (Agree? Disagree?)

2. Other than those at work, it is hard for me to think of at least two other people to whom I am accountable. (Agree? Disagree?)

3. I tend to be highly self-reliant. (Agree? Disagree?)

4. Usually, I commute to work alone. (Agree? Disagree?)

5. I often feel nagging stress. (Agree? Disagree?)

6. I often feel a sense of dread. (Agree? Disagree?)

7. I often feel anxious. (Agree? Disagree?)

8. I often feel depressed. (Agree? Disagree?)

9. I have contemplated suicide. (Agree? Disagree?)

10. I am reluctant to share my worries with others. (Agree? Disagree?)

11. There are few people in my life who I trust. (Agree? Disagree?)

12. Other than my spouse/partner or children, few people offer me personal affirmation. (Agree? Disagree?)

13. Other than my spouse/partner or children, few people offer me honest correction. (Agree? Disagree?)

14. I would say that I am not really emotionally close with people other than my spouse/partner and children. (Agree? Disagree?)

15. I expend much of my energy on pursuit of career achievement and earning money. (Agree? Disagree?)

16. I find my greatest satisfaction in my material possessions (home, car, etc.). (Agree? Disagree?)

17. In a typical month, no one besides family members visit inside my home. (Agree? Disagree?)

18. Wherever I have lived, I would usually have trouble identifying the last names of my next-door neighbors. (Agree? Disagree?)

19. Typically, outside of my workplace, I do not belong to a group that meets at least twice each month. (Agree? Disagree?)

20. Most of the time, once evening comes, I am too tired to think about getting together with other people and I would rather just "crash" in the comfort of my own home. (Agree? Disagree?)

When you are finished, take a tally of how many statements you agreed with. If you agreed with ten or more of the statements, we think you probably tend toward a lifestyle that is isolated and may be in need of new and deeper connections with others. But even if you only agreed with a few of the statements, it is important to remember that nearly all of us could stand to benefit from deeper connections with more people. If the exercise indicates that you are very isolated, don't be alarmed. While you may be too alone and independent, let's face it—you're functioning. I mean, you're reading this book. But the results perhaps bring to your awareness just how far you have drifted away from other people—people you need.

Of Glowing Monkeys and Wallpaper

As we have thought about the problem of isolation, Glenn and I have come across hundreds of different studies. Not all the research we reviewed related directly to refrigerator rights, but virtually all of it supported the idea that isolation is a pervasive and poorly addressed problem in our culture. One study we tripped upon had nothing to do with our thesis, but it amused us greatly, and in it we were able to find a useful metaphor for talking about isolation:

Scientists at the Oregon Regional Primate Research Center implanted a jellyfish gene into a Rhesus monkey. The gene in question produces a harmless protein that glows green under the right
illumination. The scientists named the monkey ANDi, a reverse
acronym for "inserted DNA." ANDi, of course, has no idea that
he glows green under certain lights. Over ANDi's lifetime the
green glow will be more or less visible depending upon the protein
production levels. Sometimes his green glow will be faint; sometimes it will be stronger. Overall, the scientists expect ANDi's glow
to increase with age.

When we read about the glowing monkey, Glenn and I laughed.
There's a parallel here between ANDi's green glow and the symptoms of isolation. Just as ANDi is unaware of his green glow, people
are often unaware of their isolated condition. Sometimes, our lives
may show only faint signs of loneliness; at other times, our isolation
may radiate from us with a force that cries out for attention.

Is this true of you? Today's lifestyle is so conducive to isolating us
from each other that hardly anyone is immune. Wherever you happen to be in your life at the moment, take a look at the problem of
isolation in your life. To what degree are *you* glowing? A little? A
lot? Not at all? Overwhelmingly? We may not notice the problem
because we live with it every day. We cope so well that the effects
seem to fade into the background.

It's like watching a baby's growth. If you're the parent, living
with the child day by day, you won't see any dramatic difference
from one day to the next. True, your child is growing and changing
constantly, but because you're with the child all the time, you don't
see the obvious. But it's different if you see the child only occasionally. I only see my grandsons every few months, and I'm always flab-
bergasted by how much they've grown and changed.

Just as the subtle changes of physical development are difficult to detect, so, too, are the gradual changes that can lead us ever so gently into social isolation. Some of these changes are so barely perceptible that we just don't notice them. Little by little, isolation becomes familiar, even normal. Sadly, even loneliness becomes like the wallpaper in your room; you don't even really notice it's there.

For example, my friend Linda lives in the same busy and densely populated New York City suburb where she was born and raised. She has well over a hundred blood relatives all living within twenty miles of each other. Other than her college years in Europe, she has only moved a few times, but always within the same local area. Whenever I'm with Linda and her husband, Don, it seems we always run into someone they know or are related to in some way. Clearly, Linda does not fit the profile of the typically dislocated individual. Yet she answered positively on eight of the twenty items on our scale. Although her family is nearby, she admitted to being highly self-reliant but also anxious and often stressed. She acknowledged having few visitors in her home each week, and she doesn't really know the people living next door to her on one side. And, ironically, when Linda and Don bought their house, they discovered that right across the street lives the daughter of her father's twin brother. Yet in the five years living there, these two first cousins have never been in each other's home. There is no animosity or family tension—just two families with separate lives, cruising along separate life orbits. They do not have mutual refrigerator rights. Regardless of who is *theoretically* available nearby, many of us are still too isolated.

Many of us are smart, well aware of the world around us, and skilled at negotiating our way through life. It is liberating, nonetheless, to be reminded that we are rarely aware of our own personal wallpaper. We see only what our experiences and circumstances allow us. When I see people in counseling, I am constantly confronted with a sad truth: Sheer intellectual capacity doesn't always lead to psychological well-being. I see too many smart people with great abilities and important careers whose personal lives are a mess. They seem shockingly obtuse when it comes to recognizing their own self-defeating attitudes and behaviors—their own wallpaper. In a sense, they are blind—just like I have been.

Helping "stuck" people to change is slow and tedious work, because too often, they cannot or will not make the necessary connections between their personal wallpaper—their assumptions, expectations, and experience—and the problems in their lives. They don't, and often don't want to, understand where they are and how they got there. Without that understanding, they can't make the changes they need to lead happier and more fulfilling lives. They need to see themselves clearly. But brother, is it hard to get the process moving! We hate to believe this, but psychological change usually happens at the speed of ketchup. And like stuck ketchup, it often takes a few jolts to get it going.

Many people received just such a jolt on September 11, 2001. Even if you weren't touched by a personal loss in the tragic events of that day, you may have discovered that you needed someone to talk to, someone to help you cope with the emotions you were feeling. If you didn't have a close friend, perhaps you found yourself talking to strangers about your own reactions. When the events of the day are unbearably heavy, the veil that covers our need to make human bonds and intimate connection is stripped away. Perhaps as a consequence of the terrorist attacks, we might begin to better understand the importance of building and sustaining deeper relationships with those around us. These relationships enrich us not only in times of intense suffering, but also in the day-to-day routine stresses that tend to incapacitate us unawares.

One final thought about the glowing green monkeys: While we may have a difficult time recognizing our own isolation and disconnection from each other such that we need to be jolted out of our state of passive stupor, it may not be so difficult for others who look at us from the outside to see things the way they really are. The TV program *Sixty Minutes II* featured a story on the September 11 terrorist attacks that left the nation reeling. In an instruction manual recovered from the personal belongings of one of the hijackers, terrorists were taught to move into relatively new neighborhoods because these were places where people didn't know each other and would be less suspicious of newcomers. A Harvard University researcher and expert on terrorism commented in the broadcast that if the terrorists knew anything about American culture, they knew how "atomistic," isolated, and detached we were as a people—and they set out to exploit that weakness for their own ends. One wonders how easy it would have been for terrorists to infiltrate our culture on such a grand scale six or seven decades ago—when people were much more likely to have a stronger personal connection with the people living next door. The terrorists found our green glow of isolation a distinct vulnerability and an appealing opportunity.

Radiating Our Isolation

For many years I knew two things about myself. As I mentioned, I have always experienced a sense of relentless, nagging stress. There always seemed to be something pending—a chain of events, some cloud on the horizon—that darkened my joy and intruded on my sense of psychological ease. I rarely felt at peace with myself. Second, I have long known that my life choices have moved me away from my family and that I have failed to make new close friends. Self-reliance, a determined individuality, and consequent isolation have characterized my whole adult life.

I knew these two things—but (maybe) like you, I kept them separate in my mind, seeing no connection between them. It was a profound revelation for me when I put them together. When I came to believe that my isolation gave rise to my anxious disposition, my perspective on life began to change. Instead of continuing my futile attempts to reduce my own stress levels (on one hand) and separately addressing my desire for more friends (on the other), I joined them into one endeavor. And that led me to a big discovery: Taking steps to repopulate my daily world with emotionally close relationships has been the single most effective force in reducing my stress levels. Refrigerator rights relationships help keep my worry levels down, moderate my anxiety, and keep my blue moods manageable.

I find my richest and most useful resource for changing my mood lies within my daily interactions with people who I'm close to and who care about me. I don't mean just my marriage, although that's obviously extremely important. Nor do I mean the sort of endless discussions of "What's wrong with me?" that we sometimes mistake for real closeness. No, I mean simply spending time in shared activities with nearby family and friends.

I discovered that being alone feeds on itself. When we don't share ourselves enough, we endure isolation without recognizing its adverse effects. Worse, we lose our sense that loneliness isn't simply to be taken for granted, again as the wallpaper of life; in fact, it's entirely unnecessary. When enough individuals feel the effects of personal isolation, it turns into a problem for the larger society. While I struggle with my own loneliness, I also see that social detachment seems prevalent in our culture.

Respondents in our research readily admitted that they failed to make the connection between a lack of happiness or peace and their disassociation from others. I'm rarely surprised these days to hear of a new study documenting an increase in socially maladaptive or unstable behavior and conclusions that associate these larger social problems with interpersonal separation and aloneness. Being alone too much of the time correlates highly with a lifestyle characterized by nagging emotional problems. Let's look at a few of these in more detail.

We Are Too Self-Reliant

Self-reliance means doing it all on your own, with no one to turn to when trouble hits. Living without refrigerator rights relationships means that we are, by default, self-reliant. And we've come to rationalize our self-reliance as a wholly admirable quality. Ben Franklin's crack that "God helps those who help themselves" endures as folk wisdom two centuries later. In fact, many actually believe it's biblical wisdom from God. We see dependence on others as a sort of character weakness. We admire our pioneer ancestors as independent, looking after themselves. And yet we forget that these self-same ancestors gathered together to raise barns, quilt, bale hay, and build houses for each other. They *knew* they couldn't do it all on their own. Why do we think we can—or should?

Our emphasis on self-reliance cuts us off from the learning and mentoring of others. On our own we insist on reinventing the wheel. Ask any psychotherapist who works with intelligent, independent, and self-reliant clients, and he or she will tell you about the emotional defenses that choke their ability to feel and seek help and counsel. When they do go to therapy because of family conflict or problems at work, the very self-reliance that they treasure in themselves often makes them resistant to the humbling experience of feeling helped. Rather than risk shame, the self-reliant endure the consequences of their poor interpersonal skills. They've built such high walls that they can't accept the necessary input to recognize and change their behavior. Therapists refer to such folks as "talking heads." I was a talking head for years.

If we are to change and grow as maturing adults, we need a steady stream of input from people we can trust. We need to receive the same rhythm of affirmation and correction that we use to raise our children. We need to feel valued by others who buttress our self-esteem. We also need to tolerate and accept correction and even criticism in order to cultivate disciplined life habits. Our character continues to evolve, not by holding fiercely to our self-reliance, but when we experience a steady diet of *both* affirmation *and* correction from people who are near and dear to us. And not just one or two people.

If we are cut off from others and cope with an exaggerated dependence on ourselves, we don't get *either* the affirmation or the correction. And this in turn further distances us from the others we need. Isolation breeds self-reliance that can deepen our detachment. We are soon left with ourselves—our worst critic and most myopic companion.

We Never Stop Moving

It's no wonder we've become so self-reliant. The daily lifestyle for millions of us has become so mobile and frenetic that we are almost never standing still. Americans are on the move daily. For instance, in 1954 only 12 percent of all workers commuted to a different county. By 1980, that figure had risen to 21 percent. In 1990, it had crept up to 24 percent. If we look at the thirty-five largest metropolitan areas in the United States, nearly 28 percent of the workforce commutes to a different county. And many more people are also commuting within the same county.

Most commuters drive to work alone, traveling in a private world. Nothing illustrates this fact quite so well as one particular failed experiment. In order to encourage energy savings and reduce traffic, the State of New Jersey, like many others set up a "commuter-only" fast lane on some highways. Any car in this high-occupancy vehicle (HOV) lane had to have at least two occupants. In New Jersey, the idea was eventually abandoned because not enough people took advantage of it—although some drivers tried to beat the system by putting a life-size dummy in the passenger seat. Think about that for a moment. People would rather pay for a dummy and enjoy their solitude than drive with a real-life passenger who they might actually get to know! Drivers reported that they wanted to be free of the scheduling constraints and pick-up arrangements that a commuter partner would require. We pursue the frenzied modern lifestyle in a dizzying spiral. We pursue our intense careers to make ever more money to pay for more things, hoping to feel ever more peaceful. In the process, we endure incredible inconvenience, steep physical and emotional costs, and family hardships.

We are simultaneously frenetic and conditioned to aloneness. One woman we interviewed talked about her strange experience of commuter privacy in San Francisco:

When I was commuting into the city every day, I became accustomed to using the HOV lanes. A system had developed in that city, where drivers who wanted the extra passengers that would entitle them to ride in the express lanes would simply pull up at designated locations and pick up waiting strangers. After three or four people piled into a strange car, you might think that conversations would begin and people would introduce themselves. Hardly. On most of the commuter rides I took, there was absolute quiet for the entire ride into the city. No one dared to break the code of silence. We were physically present for each other, but no one cared to be socially or emotionally present. It was surreal to say the least.

The failure of commuter projects to encourage carpooling is part of a larger trend toward privatization and disconnection from each other. My father worked for the gas company and commuted more than an hour each way from Long Island to Brooklyn for more than thirty years with a carpool. He spent between two and three hours each workday with the same four men. Although he considered his car mates his friends, we never met them or visited their homes and families. They remained completely separate to him and away from us.

As we go about among others in our life outside our homes, we maintain our personal thoughts and private reality. We may have lots of connections, but most rarely go beyond the superficialities of courteous acquaintance. I can be just as alone, just as isolated, while jammed shoulder-to-shoulder on a crowded bus or subway car. I just put on my earphones and dive into my book or newspaper. In many cities, there's almost an unspoken protocol that no passenger on public transit will speak to any other passenger, except perhaps to murmur, "Excuse me" while trying to snake their way to the exit. It's as though everyone on the bus is wrapped in a private membrane of disconnected reality. Let's face it, no matter who is along for the ride, commuting is typically *not* a time to build new relationships or even engage in ordinary social discourse. And modern life seems to be a nonstop commute from place to place with hardly a moment to stop and rest.

We Obsess over Our Marriages and Romantic Relationships

With so little expendable time, we focus whatever energy we do have on our few significant relationships—our marriage and our kids. Like most cultures, we value marriage above other relationships. But in many cases, our social isolation causes us to invest far too much of our energy in that one close attachment. This causes two problems: We overburden our primary relationship, and we devalue and disregard other vital connections.

In other words, we overwork our marriages and nuclear family to compensate for our loss of extended family relationships. Over the years that I have been a therapist and counselor, I have encountered more than my share of troubled marriages. When a couple comes to the point of agreeing that they need help, problems are usually significant. (I can't remember ever seeing a couple who was just looking for a tune-up in their relationship.) Most times, both parties in the marriage were ready to call it quits and were seeking counseling as a last-ditch salvage attempt. It should be a credit both to therapists and to couples that so many marriages in this desperate situation do, in fact, survive. But many do not. Young people getting married for the first time have about a 50 percent chance of divorcing in their lifetime.

Consider the statistics:

* Many first-time marriages end in three or four years. For women in the age range 25 to 29, the average (median) length of first-time marriages that ended in divorce was 3.4 years.

* Research indicates that marital distress increases the risk of physical and mental problems among the adults and children associated with the marriage.

* Marital problems are correlated with losses in work productivity—especially for males.

* The "triple threat" of marital conflict, divorce, and out-of-wedlock births has led to a generation of U.S. children at great risk for poverty, health problems, alienation, and antisocial behavior.

Complicating matters is the disheartening and all too common human tendency to spring from one bad relationship into another.

You know the expression—getting involved *on the rebound*. People in flight from a collapsed marriage immediately tumble headlong into another equally (or more!) dysfunctional relationship, without first figuring out what went wrong the last time. This baffling dynamic is what sends so many into individual therapy, mystified by their poor judgment.

But think about it: We're taught to pin all our hopes on finding that *one, true love*—you know, the one we're going to live with "happily after ever." Is it any wonder, then, that we sink so much emotional energy into our marriages? We even refer to them as our "exclusive" relationships—and in fact, this is exactly what they have become for us. We attach to our one-and-only and marginalize others. This, of course, is anything but healthy. It puts an unbearable strain on the very relationships we are trying to nurture and protect.

A relationship with one single *intimate other* to the extent that it excludes others, can never give us the complete fulfillment we crave. The soul-mate approach to resolving our sense of loneliness is a misguided value. Too great an intensity on marriage exacerbates our isolation and can even, cruelly, kill the marriage itself. We're not made to live this way.

We Are Too Worried and Anxious

It's normal, of course, to worry to some degree about our health, our finances, our children, or our jobs. The best life is never easy, and it's par for the course to be concerned about the steady stream of problems associated with jobs, kids, and money. A good quality of life demands that we keep these worries in check and not allow them to immobilize us. Sadly, this is exactly what is happening to many.

How many times in a given week do you hear the terms *stress, anxiety,* or *worry?* You probably can't count. According to Dr. Steven Hyman, Director of the National Institute of Health, "anxiety disorders are the most common mental illnesses in America. Yet many people who have them are suffering in silence and secrecy." Statistics show that about thirty million Americans suffer from one form or another of anxiety disorder. Many of these disorders can be truly disabling.

Often the specific cause of our anxiety is difficult to pinpoint. Some people feel anxious at the prospect of going through another day—yet they don't know why. I have often experienced a sense of free-floating low-grade worry that someone has dubbed *nameless dreads.* I feel anxious even as I'm aware that it is unconnected to any real threat.

Therapy and medication can help alleviate severe symptoms. But even after years of treatment (both giving and receiving), extensive study, and consultations, I still struggle with my dreads, even though I know where some of this anxiety is coming from. Why are so many of us so chronically worried, tense, and nervous? I know that like depression, anxiety is biologically based, and my makeup includes a tendency to become anxious. However, I also now firmly believe that the alleviation and management of anxiety symptoms is correlated with a strong social network—*refrigerator rights relationships.*

I am learning how my own anxiety symptoms become stronger and more difficult to handle when I struggle with them on my own. As you will see, studies consistently reveal that people without family and close emotional connections suffer worry even more, with little or no relief. Some must depend almost exclusively on prescription medication to alleviate their uncomfortable, sometimes immobilizing symptoms. So for those of us who may be biologically predestined toward an anxious mood, it is vital to know that isolation makes the tendency stronger. We need refrigerator rights relationships to help us deal with our anxieties.

As logical as this thesis is about the connection between our isolation and our anxiety, it is difficult to hold on to this basic idea in the nitty-gritty of daily life. One well-known business website (Entrepreneur.com) recently pointed out that isolation was the main reason for those hovering feelings of anxiety that just won't go away despite the fact that everything seems to be okay on face. Professor Jean Twenge, a psychologist at Case Western Reserve University, recently reported the results of her comprehensive review of studies on more than 50,000 people. The studies focused on trends that have emerged in our culture from the 1950s through the 1990s.

Twenge concluded from her investigation that there was a definite increase in anxiety throughout the culture. When she examined the studies in search of a reason for this increased worry and stress, she was surprised to learn that economic factors seemed to have little to do with it. Instead, she noted that, "Our greater autonomy may lead to increased challenges and excitement, but it also leads to greater isolation from others, more threats to our bodies and minds, and thus higher levels of free-floating anxiety." In pointing out that more of us are living alone and distrusting others, she observed that, "A general feeling of belongingness and closeness in our communities would likely decrease feelings of anxiety."

I have to tell you that in the years that we have been working on *Refrigerator Rights,* Glenn and I have been bowled over repeatedly whenever we examine the latest and best scientific evidence. We are convinced that Twenge's research is right on target and is only a sampling of the supporting evidence. Even though you may not realize it as you live it, your isolation from other people is undoubtedly related to your worry and anxiety too.

We Are Too Lonely and Depressed

Of all the possible side effects of isolation, depression would be the one we'd most likely expect to see. The core of depression is, after all, a sense of isolation and separation. Depression is such a major problem in today's life that it has left hardly anyone untouched. The statistics are nothing short of staggering. Since World War II, the rate of major depression has doubled. Over the next twenty years it seems likely to become the second most disabling disorder, right after heart disease, on the face of the planet. Some eighteen million Americans suffer from depression at any given moment. And that's just all the people with the hard-boiled, brain-based, full-blown clinical versions of the disease. How many more of us are teetering on the edge of this disorder? Therapists will readily testify that many of their patients who fail to meet the criteria for clinical depression are nonetheless suffering from milder forms of the problem.

One of the tricky aspects of depression is that the symptoms are not always obvious. We tend to think of depression as being the same as sadness or melancholy. But in fact, recognizing the symptoms of depression can sometimes be difficult, especially in children. As David Fassler, author of the book, *Help Me, I'm Sad,* says, "Some kids with depression look like adults: They're sad, tearful, withdrawn, and they have a loss of appetite and energy. But others go in almost the opposite direction: They're hyperactive, they get into fights, use drugs and alcohol, break rules, and get into trouble."

Left untreated, major depression can become life-threatening. In America, one suicide takes place about every seventeen minutes; suicide now ranks ninth as the cause of death among all people. Each suicide takes a higher, heavier toll by affecting an estimated six other people who know the victim well. Think about that statistic. If, on average, *only* six other people are affected by a person's suicide, how well connected to people was that person? In fact, one of the crucial deterrents to suicide is the sobering contemplation of how one's absence would hurt family, friends, and (especially) children.

I have never suffered a major depression, but I have experienced bouts of mild depression. When I suddenly quit my job as the host of *The Other Side,* my ill-fated NBC talk show, I went through several months of mild depression. Not only had I lost my job and role on television, but some of my dreams were also derailed. And worse, I was unsure of what to do next with my life. Before the show I had been a stand-up comedian for fifteen years. I didn't want to return to the comedy nightclubs, but I wasn't yet established as a public speaker. During this period I rarely felt sad. Instead, I was disoriented, agitated, and very irritable. I was short-tempered and unpleasant to be around. And not surprisingly, I was also very isolated. And I was, by the way, putting all my emotional baggage on the shoulders of my wife, Sally.

Within a few months of leaving Los Angeles, I began to speak and teach at companies, organizations, and churches about the problems of isolation and the need to be connected to others. When it dawned on me that I was describing my own situation, I began to make a concerted effort to reach out and be with my family. I made a point to spend more time with my brothers-in-law Jerry, Steve, and John and their families. Within a few weeks I began to feel relief and to experience firsthand how these seemingly secondary level relationships affected my mood. The depression began to lift when I reestablished some deeper connections to people.

Clearly, I now believe in the inherent link between depression and interpersonal isolation both from personal experience as well as academic study. I believe that isolation both results from and deepens a preexisting depression. People in depression desperately need to be surrounded by loving others who prop them up emotionally and watch their mood. But frequently those who are depressed report wanting only to go to bed, pull the covers over their head and be left alone. Current treatment for depression includes a combination of antidepressant drugs and supportive psychotherapy. The medication alleviates the physical symptoms of the illness by lifting your mood. Medication provides the jump-start to energize those suffering with depression to get reconnected, reversing the spiral driving them into isolation.

In times past when this revolutionary pharmacology was not available, many people depended on the surrounding support and vigilance of family and friends in their lives. Today, with so many depressed individuals cut off from family and friends, too many rely on the drugs alone or psychotherapy as a substitute for family ties. Remember, the purpose of these drugs is to give the brain a boost to set in motion a process of reengaging life. But in a culture of isolation, too many don't have a life to reengage. Consequently, some are taking antidepressants like addicts take cocaine—using the chemical to sustain their mood lift as an end in itself. This is not in sync with either the ethics or the accepted protocol for these drugs. Drugs can't substitute for a strong social network that surrounds you, affirms you, and keeps you connected and engaged. Being alone is antithetical to your mood and health.

We Are Too Rude to Strangers

Perhaps the most problematic social consequence of our isolation is our alienation from the people we *don't* know. Think about this: If I can't even stay attached to my own kin, how detached am I from people on the street?

When I go to the supermarket, I like to people-watch. I glance at others going up and down the aisles, and I remember that theoretically there's no reason why we couldn't be friends. That young woman with two busy kids in tow might be just like my own step-daughter, Tamara. That elderly gentleman checking out the lettuce could be like my uncle Ed. Each and every person I encounter is a real live human being with hopes and aspirations, disappointments, dreams, and a life I can't begin to imagine. But they are also full lives that, under different circumstances, I could enter and engage.

One of the saddest things about life nowadays is that we have no sense that we could be family to each other. Instead, we regard strangers as people with no value to us. It is this alienation that underlies what we describe in the popular culture as "incivility." What is incivility, after all, but discourtesy between strangers? In dealing with people we don't know, we may be defensive and antagonistic. Our behavior is based on the assumption that we do not and will never have a relationship with the other person. For example, when I am going about my hometown, I am far more hesitant to act out my impatience or angry frustration on the road or in a local store. But when I am in a strange city and someone cuts me off I feel freer to . . . let's just say . . . express myself. Incivility is, in essence, an attitude that accepts detachment and erases the potential for relationship. It is the plague of too many being too alone. It is a collective sociopathology.

The workplace also suffers from incivility. As researcher Martha Waggoner put it: "They're everywhere, it seems: the supervisor who walks out during an employee presentation, the manager who overrides decisions without explanation, the boss who chews out employees publicly. Incivilities such as these are becoming the norm as the ranks of the etiquette-challenged grow, warns a business professor who has spent the past four years studying on-the-job behavior."

Rudeness to strangers reaches far beyond the workplace. It often accompanies us on our drive home. Most of us notice the increased tension among drivers and are familiar with the phenomenon of "road rage." The *Chicago Tribune* offered some facts to consider:

* Aggressive driving was a factor in up to two-thirds of the highway deaths in 1996.

* Aggressive drivers are increasingly guilty of excessive speed, reckless lane-switching, tailgating, running stoplights and signs, passing on the right, honking horns and flashing lights, screaming, and making obscene gestures. The most dangerous combination is when one instigates and one retaliates—in some cases using guns, knives, or their cars to settle a dispute.

* A study by the AAA Foundation for Traffic Safety found that "violent, aggressive driving" increased 7 percent a year since 1990. One factor may be congestion. Traffic increased by 35 percent since 1987, but new roads by only 1 percent, fueling driver frustration.

The majority of people we encounter on a daily basis are strangers to us. We behave one way toward family and friends and another way toward strangers. And too often, we relate to strangers with our defenses up, ready to take offense and to retaliate. The consequences of this approach are hurting us all. Glenn made the observation that in the weeks following the terrorist attack on the World Trade Center, people on the Purdue campus seemed generally more polite and kind to each other. It was as if the tragic event had opened our eyes a bit to enable us to see that we are "all in this together" and that we really need one another to make things work. Despite our hope that this rare friendliness between strangers would persist, our ingrained behavior patterns are so strong that they pull us back to our typical styles of personal detachment. We all wish this were not so.

We Are Addicted to Distractions

In the face of our loneliness, we try to cope by turning to a wide assortment of things we think will help ease the pain. In our society we especially turn to emotional distractions like media use, recreational obsessions, or even mood changers like drugs and alcohol. What is at the root of this need for altering our consciousness?

For the young, perhaps it's about tuning into peers and turning off anxieties about fitting in and being accepted. In a society of coddled and cordoned-off adolescence, the awful pressures of peer acceptance are unprecedented. Finding a way to fit in while preserving the young person's own individuality is an overwhelming task. Now, add to this a lifestyle in which we are constantly picking up and moving, and both we and our children seem forever trying to establish new connections with strangers.

For all of us, the use of media has become a way to cope with isolation even as it deepens our disconnection. Nadine from Seattle told us of her experience:

> When we moved here for my husband's job four years ago, I was so lonely. We live in a great neighborhood in a house we love but of course we knew no one. I was home with our two preschool daughters, and the neighborhood had very few stay-at-home moms. During the day I was busy with the girls, but I got into this habit of taping two soap operas and then watching them in the evenings after supper. Even Frank started to get hooked. This was our ritual five nights a week. We even got irritated if someone called or, God forbid, dropped in to visit. It interrupted our soaps! It wasn't until we met some other couples and started to replace the soap opera routine with relationships that I realized all the time we wasted. All of those hours could have been used to meet new people. I feel like we took an extra two years to get our life started here.

It feels like none of our relationships are established, warm, and comfortable. Even when we do manage to connect with others, there's always the chance that we'll have to move again and start all over from scratch. No wonder so many kids have a desire to just feel better. Is kids' use of alcohol and drugs the result of peer pressure? Certainly this explains some of the problem. But it may also be that kids abuse these and other substances to dull the pain of isolation and loneliness.

For years as a child and a young adult, I spent so many hours—a shocking percentage of my waking life—watching television. I am a living example of using the media to distract myself from social isolation and loneliness. When I made a concerted effort to forge new relationships for myself, my television time fell off dramatically, by itself. I made no conscious effort to limit my viewing. Rather, I made the effort to be with other people. I wonder whether this same association can be made between isolation and lonely kids riveted to video games, isolated homebound people fixated on television soap operas, and solitary workers sneaking time on the job to surf the Internet? Each is spending hours engaged in a distraction instead of a relationship.

The Loss of Our Support Systems

During my travels and discussions with strangers, virtually everyone has a story to tell about being cut off and alone. They talk about a child's moving away or about relocating for a new job. And when they talk about these experiences, their feelings come quickly to the surface. They readily acknowledge their sense of loss, sorrow, and emptiness. But most of them also accept this trend as normal and inevitable. We cope with a combination of courage and denial. Frequently, people tell me about trying to maintain contact with telephone, e-mail, and occasional visits as much as their absorbed lifestyle permits. But they come to the depressing realization that their best efforts just aren't enough to overcome the distance.

Some hold on to the idea that isolation is the problem unique to the urban fast lane. I have heard many tell me that there remains a world in small towns where the problem does not really exist. I no longer believe this is true. My friend John has lived all his life in a small farm town in Nebraska, population fewer than 400 souls. He told me this story:

> Owen has been a farmer here for his whole life. Like everyone else in town, I have known him and been his friend for more than forty years. In fact, when he retired from farming about five years ago he bought the house across the street from me. Last New Year's I noticed that there were several cars in his driveway. Some I recognized as his children who had moved away, and I assumed they were having a holiday get-together. About two weeks later I was talking to another old friend who mentioned in passing that "Lena was not doing too well since Owen's been gone." I was so shocked that I just went along with her, nodding in agreement. I was too embarrassed to admit to her that I had no idea that my own neighbor had died! What kind of a world are we living in that I don't even know that my neighbor and friend died? This would never have happened twenty years ago—not here anyway. Life in the small town is not what it was.

In every corner of the society we have lost our lines of interaction with those around us. Gone are the milkman, the mailman, and the back fence. In their place are sitcoms, the national news, and the Internet. With garage door openers and air-conditioned homes we are drawn into our private domain and wave to our neighbors through our car windows as we drive down our street.

We know a lot about the larger "us" but very little about our new hometown. The noted quip by the Speaker of the House Tip O'Neil that "all politics is local," may no longer be true. A more apt paraphrase might be "all modern life is national." As Harvard researcher Robert Putnam has documented in his painstaking study of American life, *Bowling Alone,* 10 percent more Americans may be bowling today than in years past, but there are 40 percent fewer people in bowling leagues. We are literally "bowling alone." Putnam makes the case persuasively—we are cut off, we are disengaged, and we are more radically private than anyone would have ever imagined.

We don't seem to have a clue about how to address this growing sense of disconnection in our society. When Glenn and I first began collaborating on this book, we were overwhelmed by the reaction when we floated the premise of "losing refrigerator rights" past people we knew. Based on our collective experiences and concerted research, we have come to believe that the chances are excellent that you see much of your own life in these pages.

We live in a culture that beckons me to find out "who I am." It encourages my inclinations that "I gotta be me." It lures me to be in touch with my "inner child." And of course, this process of individuation is important. But many of us now need to head in exactly the opposite direction: back toward and into the lives of others. We're like hothouse pot plants that have grown and matured. But it's now time that we got set out, back into the garden.

Points to Remember

* We don't tend to connect our feelings of life stress with the fact that we have lost deep contact with our family of origin. In fact, many of the symptoms that characterize isolated people are directly tied to social disconnection.

* If we are cut off from others, we prevent ourselves from getting either the affirmation we need for a healthy self-concept or the correction we need when we wander into troubled waters. Isolation breeds self-reliance that can deepen our detachment.

* Many modern-day phenomena, including our high divorce rate; an epidemic of depression, incivility, and rudeness; aggressive driving; and reliance on drugs and alcohol are related, in part, to the steady erosion of our personal relationships with friends and family.

Part Two

How We Got Here

We Have Moved Away

Good-bye, my Fancy! Farewell dear mate, dear love!
I am going away, I know not where,
Or, to what fortune, or whether I may ever see you again,
So Good-bye, my Fancy.

—WALT WHITMAN, "Good-Bye, My Fancy"

Changing Your Address

In the first two chapters I introduced the metaphor of refrigerator rights and made the case that many, if not most of us, have drifted away from the people and places of our youth and no longer feel closely connected to very many others. You'll recall from chapter 1 that I identified three crucial cultural trends that I believe lie at the root of our isolation from each other: *increased mobility, heavy social emphasis on individualism,* and *emotionally numbing distractions.* Each of these trends is now deeply ingrained in our social structure and defies easy efforts to stem or reverse. They have become part of the air we breathe, so to speak. And as such, they are less visible and their impact more subtle. But I submit that by taking the time to understand just how deeply these factors are affecting your daily life, you will gain a new perspective on what may be ailing you emotionally and spiritually. In this chapter I want to lift the veil on something that Americans take as a commonplace occurrence: moving. While

I offered a glimpse of our mobility in the last chapter, let's take a closer look at our chronic tendency to move around.

Virtually everyone we interviewed during our research agreed: As a society, we move too much, and our moves carry a hefty social price tag. We seem to be always in transit. Before anybody could see it coming, modern society has been so rapidly and so fundamentally transformed by our mobility that we now find ourselves cut off not just from our families, but also from others in general.

When I first began to look at my own frequent moves and my loss of relationships, I thought only in terms of my own situation. It didn't occur to me that mobility might be a more general social problem. This was because my personal life was so out of the ordinary. I was a touring professional stand-up comedian, for pete's sake! Most of my friends were performers. We worked in bars and night-clubs and traveled around the country alone. This was not exactly a mainstream existence. One of my fellow comics observed, with a touch of dark humor, that we led much the same lifestyle as serial murderers. Now, there's a charming thought: Not only was I not like the Cleavers; I wasn't even like the Bundys.

Yet it wasn't until I took a break from the nightclubs and began speaking at corporate conferences that I realized that others felt the same way. As I met and talked with people who were living more traditional lifestyles, I realized that mobility and its fallout—social detachment—were affecting virtually everyone.

Data from the U.S. Census Bureau confirmed these suspicions. A staggering number of Americans move each year. According to the 2000 census, about 16.1 percent of the population—more than 43 million people—moved their residence during the census period. About 19 percent of these people moved to a different state. People aged 20 to 29 years old were the most mobile; about one-third moved in 1999–2000. Nearly 20 percent, or one in five, black or Hispanic Americans moved. For whites, the statistic was only slightly lower

(14 percent). Moving was more frequent among lower-income groups, who often must move in search of cheaper housing. Renters were nearly four times more likely to move than were homeowners.

While these statistics are staggering enough on the face of it, remember that they are only for *one single year.* Each year, the moving ritual repeats itself again, dislocating another huge number of people. Every single year, for the past two generations, about one in every seven of us moves. And there is no evidence to suggest that the trend is abating. In fact, it might be increasing as the new communication technologies evolve and once remote regions emerge economically. One disturbing trend in the most recent data from the 2000 census is that although the overall moving rate has remained about the same, people are moving longer distances. In 1998, 15 percent of all the moves made were to another state. That figure jumped to 19 percent in 2000. It seems only sensible that with longer distance moves, the probability of maintaining contact with those left behind decreases.

It seems likely that job opportunities will continue to entice companies to locate in places featuring lower taxes and cost of living. Our town is typical. Lafayette, Indiana, is a small city with a large university set in the middle of farmland. Two Japanese automakers combined to build a large plant here and now manufacture a popular sport utility vehicle. This change has dramatically transformed our community over the last decade, adding thousands of jobs, homes, stores, and people—many of them people who have moved here from other places to find jobs. The number of transplanted people increases each year, and the percentage of lifelong residents shrinks in comparison. My town is feeling the weight of these national statistics on a daily level. The sense of local connection is faltering.

The Numbers Don't Lie

Of course, the trend will continue. Another 40 million plus will move again this year, and next year, and the year after. Stop and think about the cumulative effect of this social pattern. Even if you yourself never move, what about those living all around you? In all likelihood, the constant movement of people into and out of your life has profoundly influenced your family, neighborhood, and community. You may be standing still, but the ground beneath your feet is always shifting. Perhaps a child has gone off to college, joined the Marines, or taken a better job in another state. Maybe a life-long friend was suddenly transferred to a company office hundreds of miles away. Even if you yourself haven't been "on the road," others in your life probably have been, leaving you vulnerable to the impact of our culture of geographic mobility. Sarah's account is typical:

> In the past eighteen months, my sister and her family moved away. Two months later, my best friend since high school took an overseas teaching job, and our favorite couple was transferred to the West Coast. My head is spinning. We have no close friends left. And you know what? I don't have any desire to make new ones. It hurts too much when they leave.

The bottom line is that Americans now move on average every five to six years. No wonder we lose contact with all but the most essential family relationships. Glenn and I have each tried in vain to track down childhood friends. But most of them have moved, and so have most of their families, and any leads to their whereabouts have vanished without a trace. It's a sign of the times that among the most popular features of the Internet are search engines to help us look for lost friends and family. But it isn't quite the same as driving into the old neighborhood and finding your childhood friends, parents, or aunts and uncles still living in the homes you remember. It is a sign of our age that we can reconstruct our entire family tree without ever meeting any of our kin in person. But virtual contact doesn't quite cut it.

So we have to face the music. Americans' mobility is a truism, and it's documented in the research literature. We simply take it for granted. Moving typically involves a job change: One member of the family (usually the principal breadwinner) has the chance for a better job in a different town or city. While this person becomes totally immersed in the new job, the rest of the family concentrates on creating a new home and fitting into a new life. My sister Maryellen is typical. Her husband, Dennis, is an executive with a major airline. As he climbed the corporate ladder, he has had to move at least three times. The family has learned the drill: how to pack and unpack a house, how to find a good community, and how to meet new people (join a church, attend school activities). Maryellen and Dennis have four well-adjusted kids who do well in school. The family is prosperous and happy. They know that they may have to relocate yet again in the next few years and go through the whole process yet again. Maryellen will find a new teaching job, and the children will adjust to new schools and peer groups. My brother Donald and his family have relocated at least five times for his career. My sister Barbara, her husband, Greg, and their children have moved three times, if I recall correctly. They've just told me that they are moving again to New Jersey for Greg's new job. In fact, only my brother Steve has stayed put in Rhode Island because he and his wife, Lori, are lawyers and he has an established, local practice. But even they certainly expect their kids to grow up and move away.

Today, my four sisters, two brothers, and I live in seven different states. Although your family may be less scattered than we are, this is the "family way" for tens of millions of us. Every day and everywhere the process of moving and adjusting is under way, not certainly without feeling the intense loss of loved ones. But often the initial busyness and chaos of the new move mask some of these feelings of longing for lost family and close friendships. Maryellen and Dennis, much like all my brothers and sisters, have long since become accustomed to living apart from the rest of the family.

We have heard from hundreds of people telling us their stories about moving. Some emphasized the sheer volume of their relocations. Take Martha, for instance:

Martha, the daughter of an upwardly mobile clergyman, moved four times before she was ten. After eight years in the community that "felt most like home," her family moved again. She lost all the friends and acquaintances she knew both in her hometown and in the family's summertime community. Since that time, she has moved from the United States to Canada, from Ontario to Nova Scotia, back to Ontario, and from the city to a small town. Counting on her fingers, she says that she's lived in two countries, five states, and two provinces and that she moved fifteen times before she was thirty-seven, either because of family job opportunities or in search of better or less-expensive housing. She's been settled in the same town now for fourteen years, largely "because I want my kids to have the stability I never had." But, she says, "I still feel like an air fern sometimes. I don't know if I can connect anymore. There's not a lot of point to putting down roots when they keep getting torn up again. Eventually, you just stop trying."

Other stories focused on the losses and the loneliness they felt. Estrangement from others doesn't always involve a dramatic relocation to another part of the country. We can feel our losses with any move and simply losing contact with those we have been close to in the past. Nick's move wasn't far away, but it felt like it to him.

About four years ago, my family and I moved when I took a job in another part of New York City. Our lives for the most part revolve around our children, and it is great. For at least a year or so, everything seemed fine. Both of our families are in the area and we see them frequently, so estrangement from them is not a problem. Initially I thought that moving away and blazing my own trail was the greatest thing in the world. However, after about a year or so, I began to experience periodic depression, and I gradually came to the realization that I felt estranged from what I call my "Brooklyn identity." I greatly missed my buddies from my old stomping grounds. One day it dawned on me that after we moved no one over here called me "Nick," my nickname since my days playing grade-school baseball twenty-five years ago.

I seem to have a fundamental need to touch base with my history and converse with people who knew me as a teammate, an old friend, as well as all the stories about when I overindulged at a party. My friends and I are older and we all have kids. Our conversations are less about old times and more about kids and current events. I try to make a point of visiting these old friends at a local pub about once or twice a month. Hearing them call me "Nick" and knowing that they are glad to see me is like magic for me. It seems that even a boring conversation with old friends is better than the often mundane conversations I have with colleagues, new neighbors, and parents. I'm not sure my wife feels this same way, but it's a big issue for me.

The Effects of Mobility

Relocation is a big issue for anyone, it would seem. But some may feel it more intensely than others. When I give speeches to companies and organizations, I often encounter executives and workers who have come to the United States from all parts of the world. My anecdotal observation is that when I speak about the seeming ease with which Americans move away from their families to find a better life, those who are new to the country are shaking their heads vigorously. In countless conversations with executives from other countries, whether it be China, Brazil, or India, I hear their amazement at how we marginalize and even discard our primary family relationships. Many have told me how difficult it has been to leave their own families, and they report that their principle coping strategy is to settle in cities and neighborhoods populated by others dislocated from their same homeland. There is a solid logic to this approach that recognizes the need for a strong empathic social support system, especially when you are displaced from your home culture. Somehow, many Americans don't seem to recognize the wisdom of this counsel.

People in poor but closely knit communities often face the terrible choice between working and relocating or staying put and struggling to find stable and gratifying work. Refugees and immigrants face a strange, often discriminatory environment, and they usually face it without a friendly face or someone who speaks their language. Single parents, already desperately stressed, often have to move in search of cheaper housing or better-paying jobs. If the landlord raises the rent even twenty dollars it may be too much. Once again, children particularly suffer, not just from the dislocation itself, but from the stress it puts on their families. And yet these are the people most in need of the support of friends and family, just to keep going.

The additional stresses of relocating to another culture are beyond dispute. Even within our borders, there are certain groups who experience above-average levels of stress due to isolation. Perhaps America's most painful social problem has been our inability to fully integrate minorities into the mainstream culture. To make matters worse, the present trends in corporate transfers show that minorities are more and more likely to be asked to relocate. The statistics are dramatic. During one period, from 1993 through 1997, the number of minorities asked to transfer tripled while it remained relatively stable for other groups. Who knows, perhaps this is a positive indicator of progress that minorities are joining the ranks of the leadership and executive elite for whom relocation has long been a norm. If so, this is a dubious career benefit.

If there's damage from all this mobility, it's frequently so subtle that we don't notice it. All my nieces and nephews appear to be doing fine. In all the years that my wife, Sally, was an elementary school principal, she noted that most of the newly enrolled families seemed stable, engaged, and happy. And even in those cases where kids and parents were wrestling with problems, they gave no obvious indication that relocation and detachment were significant factors in their difficulties.

The Kids Will Be Fine. Or Will They?

There is evidence that relocation does, in fact, harm children. An article in the journal *Addictive Behaviors* began: "Changing residence is a frequent life event affecting many North American children. Recently, there has emerged a growing consensus that frequent moves or recent moves may be damaging to a child's well-being at least in the short term." An article by a researcher at the U.S. Census Bureau notes that, "Americans in general have high rates of residential mobility, but American children are especially mobile

compared to children in several other Western countries and Japan."
Another researcher at Florida State University observed:

> American children today can expect to be enrolled in approximately five different schools during their educational careers. One of the reasons for this mobility is the frequency with which families change residence. In 1980, at least 7 million children were placed in new school systems as a result of their families' moving to a new residence. One-fourth of the moves in a person's life occur during childhood.

The problem isn't limited to the United States. According to a recent Canadian study, 40 percent of the parents surveyed indicated that their preschool children had moved twice during their lifetime. Nearly half of those parents reported three moves or more. The authors of this study reported that the children who moved most frequently were more likely to suffer from a variety of behavioral problems and actually tested significantly lower on objective tests of verbal ability. Of course, one possibility in a study like this one is that the children who move frequently are also children from families who are lower on the socio-economic ladder and have less education. Perhaps these factors, rather than moving, explain the lower test scores. When the authors considered this possibility by applying a number of statistical controls, they concluded that this was simply not the case. The relationship between moving frequently and lower test scores remained even after considering a child's socio-economic and education levels. They concluded that children who move frequently should be considered at risk for developmental problems—something that (we believe) parents should keep in mind when they consider making a residential move.

In our mad dash for success, good parents factor in the impact of relocation on their children. Or so they believe. Planning for our kid's future and providing the best opportunities for their success can blind us to the simple need for a stable set of attachments. Tony and Kris told us about their experience with their daughter:

> Between following the advancement opportunities in my company and changing jobs twice to climb the ladder of success, we have relocated seven times in fourteen years. I still can't believe it when I think about this fact. Our family all live 400 miles from us. Our parents are aging and missing out on their grandchildren. We finally made a decision to not take another relocation. I chose to get laid off and instead to just seek another job around here, even if it means less money and status. One of our major factors in deciding to settle was our oldest daughter's decision to not make friends anymore, because she "just had to leave them anyway so why bother." That was heartbreaking to hear from a twelve-year-old. I always knew that coping with the moves was difficult, but I never really calculated the costs of choosing career over attachments.

Maybe the damage is obvious; maybe it's subtle. But can we really expect kids to be taken away from familiar environments and put into new and strange ones *without* there being some emotional fallout?

Illusions and Miscalculations

We exaggerate the idea that moving is a great adventure, that it's fun to discover new places and meet new people. Maybe that's partly true, but what about counting the cost of all the broken ties we leave behind? In our life pursuits, we often delude ourselves about the price we will pay. It was amazing to Glenn and me how many young people fool themselves into believing that they can move away and still somehow preserve the emotional closeness they have enjoyed with their parents, siblings, extended family, and other close friends. Today, we can be productive wherever we are, and we can travel quickly and safely. We can go from one coast to the other in just a few hours. We live where we choose and expect that we can stay in touch with those we left. We believe that through visits, calls, and e-mail, we can keep our relationships strong from a distance. But most of us, if we think about it, sooner or later come to realize that we have badly miscalculated the depth and effect of the separation on our lives.

I'm only a ninety-minute flight from my parents in Atlanta. You'd think I'd find it a breeze to get together with them regularly. But they might as well be living in Europe. The cost and inconvenience of making such visits keep me from making the effort very often. I do travel through Atlanta on business trips a few times a year, and I try to visit my folks then. But my life is busy enough that it's hard to find a free weekend when I can visit. I can't seem to muster the initiative and energy it requires to stay emotionally connected to my physically distant family. In my mind, I am making the sacrifice in the service of my career.

When Sally and I were first married, she was teaching at a university in Virginia and I was still living in New York City working in the comedy clubs. In order to avoid disturbing our careers, we endured this "commuter marriage" for about a year. During that time, we made Herculean efforts to be together at every possible moment. I would fly down from New York whenever I could afford it, but most often I drove the seven hours if I could get the time off so we could be together. We spoke every night on the phone while we were apart and discussed the most mundane details of each other's daily lives. It was time-consuming and emotionally draining—a situation both of us couldn't wait to resolve. Two days after the end of her teaching semester, we finally moved in together in a house in northern New Jersey just outside New York City. The experience taught us an invaluable lesson. While we managed to remain emotionally close throughout the separation, it required an enormous commitment of time and energy. With apologies to those optimistic Internet enthusiasts (we'll get to you in chapter 5!), preserving emotional closeness throughout a long separation requires efforts that may be simply unrealistic.

I wish it weren't true, but I believe that many of us still cling to the illusion that we can pursue our careers with abandon and still hang on to family closeness. The fantasy of easy access bolsters this illusion. But too long an absence, without the prospect of a reunion in good time, can make the heart turn inward or elsewhere. And for the geographically displaced, too often it turns even more strongly toward our careers. It's not easy to face the fact: Moving tears loose the emotional webbing we need for our deepest personal health. Too often we don't understand that the most vital task we face with a move is to begin replacing that webbing by building new connections. This is not easy work, and the structure of today's society makes it tougher than ever. Let's face it—just like our town of Lafayette, your hometown is probably filling up with people and families on the move—just like you. Your new neighbors might be gone within a year. That friend you love to hang out with could be transferred tomorrow.

I am presently counseling a young mother whose husband has been diagnosed with a life-threatening illness. She was stoic throughout the interview until I innocently inquired if she had any family or close friends for support. Here she welled up with tears; she told me that her dearest friend had just been transferred out of town. She couldn't think of anyone else. I'm sure the friend hated to leave, but, like most people, she saw it as a necessity.

Why do we so readily surrender any sense of stability and permanence? Do a quick inventory in your head and count the names of family members and friends who are alive and well and prospering—somewhere else. Calculate those who once shared refrigerator rights but who are now gone from your daily life. And for each of these moves you made away from these important people, what was the reason for the relocation?

Compelled to Move

For many of the people we interviewed, their moves, although a voluntary act, were usually done with the intent to search for a better life. They felt compelled by job opportunities to change places and resettle, although, in fact, nothing was forcing them to do so. It was a choice; moving wasn't really a necessity. This is true in my case. Every time I relocated, it felt like something I just had to do. I suspect that for most of us, a decision to relocate felt necessary at the time.

In some cases, of course, a move is an urgent necessity. It is not a choice but an economic or emotional imperative. And often, the people for whom a move is necessary are the very people who are in most need of the support networks they're forced to leave behind. One woman told us of having to leave an abusive relationship she was in for eight years:

He had taken so much of my life, and I had finally had enough. My only chance for an escape was to move away from Washington, the only home I had ever known. My older sister relocated to Texas about six years earlier, and she offered to help me. The rest of my family, two sisters and a brother, all married with families, and my parents remain in Washington. All of my friends from work and school, with the exception of one, are all there as well. I have just recently started making friendships, mostly through work. But there is only one person locally who has refrigerator rights at my new apartment, and that is my sister. I don't think I will ever regain friendships and relationships that happened throughout the twenty-five years of my life. How do I calculate the extent of this loss? It was never my desire to move.

Many people have told us that they felt trapped by their families and wanted to get away. And for some of us, there is an odd illusion afoot that the freedom to elect our own associations, to choose our relationships, is somehow preferable to being tied to our own kin. Over time many came to realize that while they still believe that leaving their own family was a good thing, they never really completed the other half of the equation, reattaching to others to form a new family, establishing a new group of refrigerator rights relationships. Paul told us his account:

My mother moved us a lot when I was growing up, usually to hide from my father. He was always trying to get custody or visits with my two brothers and me. Obviously, she didn't trust him. Eventually, we ended up in Orlando, and I've lived here since I was in junior high school. My mom's immediate and extended family all live in Delaware while my father's family all come from Canton, Ohio. I have always felt stuck in the middle of these two estranged families by more than just a thousand miles.

I have since established my own life with a wife, job, and kids. I really love Orlando and have no desire to leave, although there are times I feel it would be nice to have some family closer. I am really not that close with anyone outside of my wife and children. I have guys I meet for golf occasionally, but no one with whom I can share the feelings and thoughts we all have. I don't want to move; I want to enjoy my home and the memories we are making for many years to come and stay put, even if it means losing contact with my family and my roots. But getting new relationships that feel like family members has never happened for me. There are times I don't think it ever will.

If you have been a part of the *moving to get away* crowd, you have surely experienced the chaos, stress, and social isolation that moving exacerbates. But there is some relief in there, too—relief from the negative effects of a demeaning boss or a hurtful family member. But the act of moving as an escape can actually serve as a disincentive for making new relationships. If you know that you're likely to pull up stakes in a couple of years, you don't have much motivation to become an active member of your community. Making friendships may seem like an act of futility. At the same time, this turning away from closeness in our present life only deepens the longing we feel for contact with our lost relationships from the past. It's ironic, but we often feel more psychologically attached to cousins who we never see than we do to the people in the next house or at the next desk. Even though nearby neighbors share our daily life, we often keep them at arm's length. We're left with a sense of longing because of our social detachment. In their book, *Contemporary Social Problems,* three sociologists recently noted that Americans today experience twice as many transitions as in the recent past. Today, Americans can expect to go through an extended period of living away from their family before marriage. They are also far more likely to separate from their spouses or get divorced and to remarry—with an even higher probability of divorcing again. Families, like society itself, seem to be increasingly fractured.

At the same time, new technology—especially the Internet—continues to revolutionize every facet of our lives. We have achieved new heights of productivity, and there's more to come. In just a few short decades, air travel has exceeded our wildest fantasies. We are no longer held captive to one physical location as our grandparents were only a few decades ago. We take vacations in exotic places. We have more entertainment choices than any people who have ever lived on the face of the earth. We can see and hear every wonder of the world sitting before our computer screens in our pajamas. It's a great time to be alive. So what's wrong? I believe that one thing that's gone wrong is that we have too easily accepted the necessity to relocate. And once relocation happens (either by us or to us), we have too often failed to think through its consequences and pursue a determined course to counter its effects on our relationships and our personal health.

But geographic mobility is not the only thing that has beset us. In our culture, we celebrate the individual. Our heavy emphasis on individualism manifests itself in the rigorous course we set for ourselves to succeed. We set off in the pursuit of happiness. We set off for success. And our dogged striving is deepening our isolation and making matters worse. Our striving is making it harder to reclaim our refrigerator rights. Just as this chapter has examined the mobility theme in more detail, the next chapter focuses more closely on our hearty appetite for success.

Points to Remember

- Nearly forty-five million Americans move every year. The average American moves every five to six years. This huge volume of geographic mobility has had an untold impact on the social fabric of daily life by rupturing our most significant relationships with family and friends.

- We too easily accept the premise that we must move in order to follow a career or get away from family—and we tend to delude ourselves about our ability to remain in contact with those we leave behind.

❖ The downside to relocation is subtle—but that doesn't mean it is trivial. We underestimate the impact of our moving around, and we pay a huge emotional price for this miscalculation—the price of lost relationships.

4

We Are Always Striving to Succeed

Movin' on up . . .
to a deluxe apartment in the sky.

—*The Jeffersons* theme song

In Search of My Wonderful Life

What do we need to satisfy us? Is it succeeding? Is it getting to the top of our careers? Is it raising children who surpass our own dreams? Is it achieving enough so we can say "if my friends could see me now"? Surely no one sets out expecting to fail, even if our fears tell us we might. The goal is always to succeed—at something. And it is with this in mind that we go forth in life. In America, our old heritage of "rugged individualism" has spawned a culture that is wildly driven to succeed—sometimes at any price. This drive to achieve and succeed goes hand-in-hand with geographic mobility. We'll move in order to succeed. Let's look more closely at our willingness to pay any price—including losing our refrigerator rights relationships—in order to climb the career success mountain.

In the film *Superman,* after the death of his adoptive father, young Clark Kent realizes that he must leave home. As the young man and his elderly widowed adoptive mother stand in a windblown Nebraska wheat field, she says sadly, "I knew this day must come . . . where will you go?" Clark turns toward the horizon and replies simply, "North." With that he sets off for the frozen Arctic, where he will find himself and establish his life's mission. This romantic notion touches a chord in every adolescent who approaches that transitional moment into adulthood. It is a traditional rite of passage for young adults to strike out on their own and find their way in the world. Although this has always been true, it has never been more literally true than today. We are beckoned out of our families toward a life of our own. It's cause for both sadness at the going and celebration for the new independent life.

In times past, however, this transition did not necessarily entail leaving one's hometown or proximity to family. Although we traditionally celebrated the courage of those who ventured out into the unknown, these stout souls were the exception. Most folks stayed home or near home.

The new norm is that our children will set off on independent adventures to far-off places, most often following career opportunities. The trend now is that even long before marriage, the words of Genesis apply: "a man shall leave his mother and a woman leave her home." When I left home and went away to college, as much as I longed to find the love of my life, I also felt a strong desire for my independence. In fact, I couldn't wait to get off on my own. Like many adolescents, this longing had little to do with realism. I craved personal autonomy, but I was pretty foggy about personal responsibility or the skills I'd need for survival. In my zeal for freedom, it never occurred to me that I might not hack it by myself.

Who among us can't relate to the itch to get up, get out, and go, even if we don't know where we are going? We seem culturally conditioned to strike out. Whether it's graduation, our wedding day, or a trip to the recruiter's office to sign those enlistment papers, each of us faces that take-off moment. And each of us must come to terms with how our fantasies confront the (sometimes stark) reality of making a life on our own.

For millions of us, a large part of what motivates us seems to be an urge to get away from where we have been. Why are we so restless, not content to remain where we began or settled? Are we so eager to find something better that we're willing to let go of whatever we've got in the way of home and stability? Are we being pushed or pulled? What are we seeking? Do we even know? We already discussed some of the facts about mobility in the last chapter, but it begs the question, *why* do we move? One of the powerful forces urging us along is our individualism and the urgent quest for success and power.

The U.S. Constitution speaks of our rights to "life, liberty and the pursuit of happiness." But what is happiness? In popular culture it seems to be defined in terms of career and material success, respect, and influence. We realize that this is how people from other cultures often view us, and we sense their mild (or not so mild) disdain for our values. From the outside, Americans seem to be driven by exactly these goals that bear a striking resemblance to the life of celebrity and fame. It seems that we are in hot pursuit of cash, comfort, and cachet. We crave personal significance. Are we really this superficial? Are our goals really this crass? Have we really become a society of obsessive strivers? It seems almost too simple.

There is nothing new about the human urge to achieve. But a number of factors unique to modern culture have worked together to prod us—to propel us up, out, and away in the "pursuit of happiness." A combination of economic opportunities, advances in science and technology, and (especially) electronic media seduce us away from what seems to us to be a monotonous, irksome, or confining reality. The possibilities seem endless. The cultural sirens sing so seductively: *You can be anything you want. You can do anything you want. Be all you can be.* And who among us has the backhanded courage to say, "No, I'd rather stay right here, thank you very much"?

The Lure of the Ideal

The price of our geographic mobility is tangible and concrete. Although many of us seem oblivious to it, we pay a price when we move away or when others we care about leave us. It would be nice to think that in return for the sacrifices we make, the benefits of our success would be equally tangible and concrete. Unfortunately, that may not be the case at all. Sometimes our pursuit is more ethereal. We are chasing dreams and fantasies that will forever elude our grasp. For instance, often in the middle of a harsh Midwestern winter season I yearn for the pleasant southern climates. I dream out loud about moving to Florida or back to California—new careers, new possibilities, no snow-shoveling. . . . My better judgment tells me that this is impractical. We'd be cutting ourselves off from friends and family. But in fact, we *could* up and move fairly easily. Perhaps many of us do take the bait to leave because it has become so easy for us.

Some move for lifestyle reasons rather than for career reasons. The goal is a better life, even at the expense of the relationship losses it will incur. Every year, millions of retirees and seniors gravitate south to a warm and open environment such as Florida or Arizona. Others opt for a chance to pursue certain activities such as golf or skiing. Dan moved from Albany, New York, to Los Angeles because he had ambitions to become a film editor. He didn't have a job, but left anyway because he wanted to be near the hub of the entertainment industry. John moved away from his small Arkansas hometown to Philadelphia because he felt more comfortable and accepted as a gay man in a large city and more connected to a supportive community. Jenny left Fort Lauderdale and settled in Michigan after attending college there, because she wanted to live where there was a change of seasons. In one way or another, every one of us strives to do what we want and to be where we think we can experience life, liberty, and happiness.

Strangely, the one dream that does not seem to tug us in a new direction is the dream of reconnection. Despite the fact that none of them had very many refrigerator rights relationships, the notion of moving back home for the purpose of reconnecting seemed quaint and essentially humorous to the people we interviewed. This is true for most of us. I cannot imagine my family reconvening in Brooklyn, New York, anytime soon. We did meet a few individuals who did just that, like the man who took a big step backward in his career as a museum curator in a large southern city to return to his hometown in Indiana. He voluntarily gave up his salary and expense account to run a small-town historical society near the family he had left twenty years before. But he is definitely more the exception than the norm.

For the young career-minded person, the dream of an independent lifestyle and a successful career is usually far more attractive than the more ordinary benefits of living close to family. We take it for granted that personal lifestyle preferences trump deep, stable relationships. We found very, very few people who stayed in a place that they disliked in order to remain near their families. It seems we are first and foremost in pursuit of personal happiness that we think comes from individual achievement, not deep relationships.

We've spent a lifetime being blitzed by media messages that define for us the norms of success and happiness. Sandwiched between the commercials that shamelessly promote material accumulation, we watch hour after hour of programming that depicts people wrestling with problems of relationships and the pursuit of peace and happiness. It's in the nature of the media to depict these characters' lives as richer and more exciting than our own. We're always being shown the possibilities in fantastic other places. To this day, I remember longing to be in Southern California as, on a cold winter Saturday, I watched the Rose Bowl in Pasadena. I wasn't only fantasizing that I was a sports star; I wanted to get away from where I was living. It may be hard to believe, but kids in Hawaii also feel the itch to get off their own island. I think this is a cultural value that is bred into us early. "The grass is always greener": That's what we're now trained to believe. To really succeed, I have to go off and do it my way.

I Order You to Strive

Good families put a strong emphasis both on achievement and on serving the community. In my own family, I was not encouraged to wander aimlessly. My parents emphasized personal responsibility and service to others. There was no compromise for us. In my restricted social climate I learned early on what kind of life I was meant to lead. I would grow up to be obedient, go to college, become a man of faithful character; and, therefore, I would succeed. This was the essential life plan for everyone in my house. I squirmed to get loose, but I ultimately conformed. I became a fairly compliant striver in search of my fulfillment.

Ambition is always aimed high. I never had much yearning for a life unloading trucks or digging holes, although I have done both. One of my jobs during college summers was digging up streets in Brooklyn for the gas company. The jackhammer I used weighed almost as much as me, and it took all my strength to avoid bouncing down the street like a runaway motorized pogo stick. Three summers of this was enough for me. As a kid, my ambitions were the same as most others in my social class. I wanted fame and riches, in that order. From my earliest years, I noticed the disconnection between the decent, fulfilled life that my parents and teachers were preaching and the life being shown on TV and in the movies. Even when programs depicted worthy life pursuits, I clung to my cheaper ambitions. *Room 222,* a program about high school life, didn't inspire me to become a beloved teacher; it merely deepened my desire to become a Hollywood star. Even in my tender youth, I knew that actors got rich and teachers made peanuts. When professional athletes were interviewed on television, it was perfectly obvious that many were virtually illiterate. But the ballplayer drove away from the arena in a Porsche, while every decent, articulate man in my neighborhood pulled out of his driveway in a Chevy Nova. Three guesses which lifestyle got my attention.

Getting ahead and becoming successful always felt more like a probability than a mere possibility to me. My drive to attain has never gone away, and I sometimes wonder if this passion will ever subside. Here I am, past middle age, yet still hacking away at my career. I'm not just working; I'm striving. I'm yearning. I'm pushing myself to make it. I'm still hard at the pursuit of happiness. Glenn is a dedicated striver as well. He's a few years younger than I am, but he has no expectation that his passion for success will abate any time soon, either. Where I spent my youthful summers with a jackhammer, Glenn spent his in the back kitchen of his parents' donut shop squirting jelly into empty donut shells. Across several years and millions of donuts, he grew determined to become more successful.

This zeal for our children's success has had an enormous impact on society over the last sixty years or so. In 1940, for example, fewer than 5 percent of people 25 or older had attended four years of college. Today, the percentage has increased to nearly 25 percent—a five-fold jump. While increased access to college is something to celebrate, the phenomenon buried in the statistics includes the unwitting encouragement to separate our children from their families. College spurs children to leave home, frequently for schools that are a long way away. And you know they typically move on to jobs that are distant from their homes and families. So while college represents a wonderful life-changing opportunity, it also presents a serious challenge to the preservation of close family relationships. Like a stint in the military, college is an important transition, starting us on a life of moving away and going out on our own. And it virtually assures our detachment from our family and place of origin.

Although I believe that the value of striving is deeply ingrained in each of us and is self-evident in many ways, I also believe that there are cultural indicators at every turn that point out the futility of this value. The pursuit after success and its desired rewards is perhaps the clearest manifestation of the American myopia about striving for achievement and power. While we will address the problem of materialism in detail in chapter 6, suffice it to say, there is plenty of evidence that "materialism" is a pernicious problem in our contemporary age. In one study, the researchers actually found that the most materialistic individuals were the ones who were *least satisfied* with their current standard of living. The dark side of the striving mentality is that it seems to doom us to a life of dissatisfaction and a constant longing for more.

Confessions in Naked Ambition: A Case Study in Striving

I know a lot about the constant longing because most of my adult life has been a story of striving for success—looking for the brass ring. Perhaps it might help if I shared with you a bit of my personal experience about the pitfalls of being fiercely oriented toward individual personal striving. Perhaps you'll catch a glimpse of yourself and others you know in my story.

I spent fifteen years, from 1979 through 1994, as a professional nightclub comedian. I traveled the country working everywhere and with everyone else on the circuit. The fact that you have never heard of me tells you something of my experience. Just the same, even without breaking into national fame, I was in the stand-up trenches for a long time.

When you become a professional comedian, the ultimate goal is clear as a bell: You are trying to get famous and rich and powerful, in that order. There are no illusions that you are doing something to benefit the world, no bromides about "bringing the joy of laughter to others." If it happens, that's nice, but comedians are first and foremost career-strivers. Of course, good comedians truly *love* to make people laugh. It's a great high to stand in front of several hundred strangers and hear a roar of hysterical laughter at your observations. There's nothing like it.

I started doing stand-up when I was twenty-nine years old. I began my career at a place called Richard Dixon's White House Inn. This was a tacky little shack off the highway exit into North Massapequa, Long Island, that had been converted into a comedy nightclub. The proprietor was "Richard Dixon," a thoroughly unique individual who remains a legend among stand-up comedians. Dick, whose real name was Jim LaRue, was an advertising executive who bore a startling resemblance to President Richard Nixon. Sensing a golden opportunity, in 1968 he left his job and began a new career as a presidential imposter. It was a great gag and a lucrative career while it lasted. Unfortunately, the Watergate scandal ended more than just Richard Nixon's career. Dick Dixon, his gravy train derailed, took his cash and opened up a club for aspiring comedians.

The comedy club craze was about to explode, and Dixon was a pioneer. As quirky and overbearing as he could often be, Dick was great to brand-new talent. He gave you a chance, stage time, blunt critique, and encouragement. The gang of comedians hanging around his club every night teased him mercilessly. To this day, any veteran comedian who started in the 1980s on Long Island can still do a drop-dead impersonation of Dick Dixon's animated gestures and gravelly, gunshot voice.

For several years, Dixon's club drew a packed crowd who paid to drink and watch about fifteen comics-in-training. They laughed, groaned, and heckled the night away watching the inept, the pre-destined, and the hungry. On my first night there, the lineup included (among others) Eddie Murphy, Rob Bartlett (now with the *Imus* radio program), and Bob Nelson, long before his many HBO specials and *Tonight Show* appearances. The environment was a contrast between the humility of being heckled in this anonymous little bar and the electricity of chasing after the classic American brass ring: fame, riches, significance, and power. I was intoxicated and couldn't wait to climb the show business ladder in stand-up comedy.

I had no illusions about how difficult it would be, given the nature of the profession, the work environment, and the ferocious competition. Every aspiring comic hanging out at Dixon's and the other comedy clubs shared one single dream: to develop a routine funny and polished enough for *The Tonight Show* with Johnny Carson. Carson was the end game, the gateway to your fame and fortune. Our role models included everyone who was Carson-level: Bill Cosby, Robert Klein, Joan Rivers, Rodney Dangerfield, and George Carlin. Those right ahead of us were comics like Jerry Seinfeld and Paul Reiser. And we were all very, very hungry. All professional comedians are obviously scrambling for success. But when I began speaking to leaders and employees in corporations and organizations, I noticed that they were all playing the same success game, albeit more subtly. The sales executive knows what the pinnacle of success is for his career. The marketing professional knows exactly where she wants to be. So does the engineer, the baggage handler, and the manager in training. Ask anyone who is striving, and they can tell you what position they dream about having and the lifestyle that goes along with it.

Starting out as a stand-up comic, you need a day job to pay the bills. My first day job was substitute teaching. This ranks somewhere between telemarketing encyclopedias and summertime roofing in Arizona. It made me pine for the good old days digging ditches in Brooklyn. The kids gave me my first glimpse into my latent homicidal impulses. Fortunately, after a few months I was rescued: I got a full-time teaching job at a local Catholic high school. During my interview, the principal regretted that he couldn't pay me at a level equal to my doctoral degree. I told them I was more interested in teaching seniors than I was concerned about a salary. This was not quite the truth. What I really wanted was to keep my class preparations down to a minimum and to preserve my energy for performing every night. He agreed to my request, and I was assigned five classes of senior English.

So began a peculiar two-year routine. I would teach all day and then race home to sleep for about four hours each afternoon. I would wake up about 8:00, shower, and get to Dixon's for the evening show. Sometimes, if I had an early spot, I could be finished by 10:00. But many nights, especially at the very beginning, I was drawing performing spots like 12:15 or 1:05. Either way it didn't matter much because, regardless of what time I performed, all the comedians would hang out until after the show ended. And most nights we would then hit an all-night diner for breakfast. Was I neglecting my students? Who's to say? However, I was voted teacher of the year. But it clearly indicates my fervor for success—even at the price of my daily happiness and lifestyle.

After two years of night crawling, I had developed an act that was good enough for full-time performing work. When I finished the 1982 school year, I had solid bookings in nightclubs through the fall. I was now a professional stand-up comedian. Like all professional comedians, I was either the show's MC or the opening act. To get the headliner's slot (and pay!) you needed an hour of solid material. Headlining would come later. My first out-of-town booking was a great thrill. After hundreds of late-night spots, performing in front of a handful of drunk and tired club prowlers, I found myself with a booking at a Pittsburgh comedy club. I was booked as the MC; T. P. Mulrooney, from Chicago, was the middle act, and Jay Leno was the closer.

Even though he was not yet generally famous, Jay was a star among comedians, a prolific writer with an edgy onstage persona. Best of all, offstage he was a real sweetheart to new comedians. And Jay defined perseverance. He'd been working in comedy for well over a decade, surviving rejection (he'd been dropped from *The Tonight Show,* and sitcom producers rebuffed him because they said he didn't "look right" for television) but still pursuing his dreams. And here he was plugging away in Pittsburgh. What was, for me, a major step up was, for Jay, the basement. But his spirits never seemed to flag. We admired him to no end.

One Friday night, we were sitting backstage at the club between shows, and T.P. was asking Jay's advice. Of course I was all ears. Jay asked, "How long have you been working?" T.P. said, "About five years." "Okay," Jay said, "so by now you've just about figured out who you are onstage. Once you get a sense of what your onstage persona is, you then need to work at it for another five years or so." Jay estimated that it took about eight to ten years of full-time work to make a comic ready for the big time. Oh brother! And here I was, thirty-one years old, with only a couple years of experience.

The only thought that made another eight years endurable was the camaraderie, the relationships. I had already been through the roughest early years alongside the other struggling comedians. As different as we were, we had a great bond of friendship because of our shared experiences in the clubs on the late-night scene. I was always surrounded by my performer friends, all heading in the same direction as me. We were striving for individual success and the fulfillment of our dreams, but we were doing it together.

In retrospect, it's amazing how determined we all were, enduring the hardships unique to nightclub performing. Imagine being in front of a few hundred strangers, some of them drunk, many of them anywhere from skeptical to hostile, lying in wait for you to prove how unfunny you are. And you get up in front of this crowd and fail night after night. You keep this up until slowly you stop failing. This is why comedians arm themselves with stock lines to defend themselves from heckling: "Hey pal, this is my job. Do I come to where you work and tell you when to flip the burgers?" Or you point to the heckler and say to the crowd, "You know, this is why some animals eat their young." Usually the audience is with you and roars their approval at the retaliation. Don't listen to anyone who says that comedians really like hecklers or that they help the act. This is a lie from the pit of hell. I laughed out loud when my friend and fellow comic Jim Myers recently wrote an article for our online comedians' magazine titled "Why Hecklers Must Die."

In the middle of my climb up the show business ladder, my life began to unfold in other directions. I had met Sally a few years before starting as a comic. We both worked for the Massachusetts Department of Education, but in different departments. Shortly after we met, she moved to Indiana to start her Ph.D. at Purdue University. We kept in touch by letter and phone, and our relationship grew. It was slow growth—exactly what I needed, given my fear of becoming impulsively involved too soon after my divorce. Sally and I became friends over the course of four years. She finished her degree and took a teaching position in Virginia just as I was starting full-time performing.

Even after we got married and moved in together, we might as well have been in separate states. By 1986, I was beginning to get work as a headline comedian. I was on the road about forty weeks of the year, making progress in my act and gaining a reputation in the nightclub business. But as you can imagine, such a career is not conducive to a stable home life. It was becoming clear that our lifestyle was not satisfying either of us. Sally worked days during the week, and I worked at night. In addition, we were becoming more involved in our church, and my faith was beginning to become increasingly important to me. I began to think about getting out of stand-up comedy.

I hated to give up my dream of making it in comedy, even though I knew that this was the right decision. Comedy had been the focus of my ambition for six years. I'd worked incredibly hard, and I'd loved the life. And now, here I was, thirty-six years old and contemplating yet another career change. I began to have doubts about my character and resolve and worried that I was blinking in the face of success. Maybe really making it was too threatening for me. But despite my own self-doubts, I couldn't deny the spiritual awakening I was experiencing.

I had a calling. Like many ministers, I feel a bit shy about trying to explain the experience of a call to nonreligious people. I'm never sure if there is secular vocabulary that does justice to the moment. I didn't hear a voice, and I wasn't in an otherworldly state. But in the middle of conversation with a family friend who himself was attending seminary, I felt a particular moment of absolute, compelling certainty that this was what I was to do. The feeling was profound. It's wasn't anything like "Hey, that would be a good thing to do"—in fact, it *wasn't* a good thing to do from a career standpoint. A call isn't a choice rooted in logic, nor is it always the culmination of a career path. Quite the contrary: My stand-up comedy career was going well, and I had every reason to believe that I could make it. I had a terrific act and the right look for television. And here I was, getting yanked in quite a different direction . . . I acknowl-edged my spiritual experience and began to investigate studying for the ministry.

At first I tended to see my two careers as being separate and con-tradictory—that a career in comedy/show business was directly op-posed to a calling to the ministry. But then it dawned on me that I might be able to have my cake and eat it, too. Seminary meant day-time classes. Seminary students also have to eat. As a comedian I worked at night. I, therefore, had a perfect job for attending school full-time. Thank you, God.

And this is exactly how it happened. I began as a full-time stu-dent at Union Theological Seminary in New York City. Shortly af-ter beginning seminary I heard about a joint program that Union ran with Columbia University's School of Social Work. It would add another year of graduate studies, but I knew this was what I needed to do. So for four years I attended classes each day and re-turned home to have dinner with Sally and tell her about what I'd learned in school. I would then shower, change clothes, and drive to a comedy club somewhere in the area to do a show. There were plenty of comedy clubs in the metropolitan New York area, and I could work regularly every week. I'm certain I was the only student enrolled in a systematic theology class anywhere in the world who was also performing at Going Bananas Comedy Club.

I would only take out-of-town gigs on school breaks and during the summer. My fellow comics got used to seeing me slogging through Aquinas, Plotinus, and Kant backstage between shows. I averaged about four hours of sleep a night but was feeling more en-ergized and emotionally fulfilled than ever before. I still had no idea how I was going to blend or reconcile my diverse career interests. That would evolve over time.

After being in comedy for fifteen years, the experience I gained was amazing. When I became first a minister and next a therapist, my life took curious new twists and turns. But looking back, my career path has been fundamentally a story of striving. Your experience may be similar. Most of us are trying to make our work life and our personal life fit together into a seamless whole. We are trying to be productive and hold on to a positive mental attitude and all the while reassure ourselves that this path is the right one for success.

Whether it's Bill Gates's Microsoft or Fred Flintstone's stone quarry, whether it's a traditional family model or some patchwork collection of adults and kids making a family, happy people live productive lives. And that's what most of us are striving for—to be productive and find emotional and spiritual fulfillment. For some of us—perhaps most of us—it seems that too often our obsessive focus on producing perpetually postpones the fulfillment.

The Price We Pay

We all begin with dreams and fantasies of a career that will give us respect, rewards, and influence. But like me, I'm sure that you have had to make unforeseen adjustments and decisions that took you to places you never planned or imagined. And most likely your path has precipitated times of separation from your home, family, and friends. You have very likely lost many of your refrigerator rights relationships. Career opportunity almost always wins out over connection to cousins.

The current cultural norms are clear: We should not impede our grown children, adult siblings, or aging parents when they relocate in order to fulfill a life's goal. While we acknowledge the daunting adjustments and dread the emotional "good-bye," these are matters that require coping, not rethinking. We wouldn't dream of uttering the words we long to say, words like, "Oh please don't go," or "Stay here, we're more important than some great job opportunity." Sad as it is, we expect them to go, and we accept their departure. Dispersal and separation are the rule.

For myself, looking back, I grossly underestimated the impact of always choosing career over commitment and stability. I now see it as a skewed value. But at the same time, turning down opportunities to advance my career threatens my chances for achievement and is out of sync with the new norms of striving. In hindsight, I must admit that I have paid a high emotional price for my career ambitions. I sacrificed stability and suffered with the anxiety that goes along with taking high-wire career risks.

I was always focused first on the goals of my career—success in show business. All other matters, including relationships with family and friends, followed in priority. My view (unconscious, of course) was that family and other relationships were there for background support and enjoyment. It didn't occur to me until much later that it could or should be the other way around. The purpose of career ambition is to enable a life of emotionally close relationships. Whether it involves sustained connections to my own kin or a re-created network of new relationships, attachment to others is the end game in human living.

I suppose my life story has been more chaotic than most. But so many other people I know, including those who have followed a more traditional career and life course, have ended up feeling as I did—too cut off from others. I might have moved more often than Glenn has, but he is not much more connected to his family. I may have had more career changes, but he is not much less restless and mobile than I am. I'm not the only one who feels like I'll never quite arrive. Many are looking for what's better, what's next. This is the new standard—all in the name of striving. I often find myself singing the U2 song that goes, "I still haven't found what I'm looking for."

How do we cope with the losses we experience as a result? We are keeping ourselves distracted as a way of avoiding feelings of loss and loneliness—the price we pay for all our moving and striving. Modern life offers plenty of such distractions. First and foremost, we have our media and their all-consuming magic. And that's what we'll look at next.

Points to Remember

❖ The frenzy of relocation in our culture is tied deeply to our value of individualism and our desire to make our lives into success stories. Unfortunately, the price we often pay for following these values is the loss of essential relationships that we require in order to be healthy.

❖ While we delude ourselves about the price of moving on our relationships, we also see our striving after success as a striving after concrete and tangible gains. However, just the opposite is often the case. Much of our mobility comes in pursuit of things that are less than tangible, more ethereal, and more likely to elude our grasp.

❖ Strangely, while we dream after all sorts of career success and material gain, the dream of deep and intimate connections with other human beings doesn't seem to tug at us to the extent that it compels us to change the way we live. We tend to think that career goals come first, while family and friends are there to fill our background. Instead, career ambition should be focused on enabling us to better connect with others. Attachment is the "end game" in human living.

5

We Substitute Media for People

Most people are still blissfully ignorant of what the media do to them; unaware that because of their pervasive effects on man, it is the medium itself that is the message, not the content. The content or message of any particular medium has about as much importance as the stenciling on the casing of an atomic bomb.

—Media visionary MARSHALL MCLUHAN

In the last half-century, we have lived through a colossal media revolution. Even if you're younger than I am and have no memory of life before cable television and computers, the explosive advance of technology means that you have your own "media boom" story to tell. For me, it was the introduction of color television. For you, it might be DVD players or the Internet. For my grandsons, it could be holographic television or surgically implanted wireless phone chips.

Electronic media in all its forms present a far different challenge to the quality of our life today than it did a few decades ago. We used to hope that the easy availability of information would make us more efficient, more informed, and more connected. But in fact, we're now starting to see that our gadgets only make us more self-absorbed. Electronic media present a different, deeper challenge to us now than they did when they first arrived. Add the numbing dis-

traction of electronic mass media to the dangerous brew of geographic relocation, and striving for independence and the formula
for lost refrigerator rights is all but complete.

Glued to the Tube

No one has to tell you that the media, especially television, have
had a profound effect on you and me and our society in general. We
may not be able to say with certainty how it has changed things, except that most of us have a nagging sensation that its impact has
probably been more bad than good. I hope in this chapter that I can
shed some light on what we believe has been one of the media's
most telling effects: the acceleration and perpetuation of the loss of
refrigerator rights relationships due to its distracting power.

The boom decade for TV in the United States was 1950–1960.
In 1950, for example, only 10 percent of households had a TV set.
By 1960, that figure had jumped to 90 percent. For all practical purposes, virtually every home now has a television—in fact, more
homes have televisions than indoor flush plumbing. Shocking, but
in fairness, if my own parents had said to us, "You kids have a
choice—an indoor bathroom or a television set. You can't have
both, which will it be?" our instant reaction would have been,
"Duh! Turn on the tube!"

Glenn teaches a large lecture class, an introduction to mass communication. He always asks his students in the course how many
TV sets their families have at home. Each year that he's surveyed his
class, the average number has increased. It's no longer unusual to
have many students report that their home has four or five TVs.
The record number of sets reported was fourteen! He also asks
them to report where the sets are located. One student reported
that his family had TVs in two of the household's bathrooms.

The astonishing growth in the number of TV sets is only one indicator of the lure of this medium. About 70 percent of the country now has access through cable systems to large numbers of channels. Projected future cable systems will carry literally hundreds of channels. Premium services and pay-per-view options now offer movies all day and all night. With the digital revolution upon us and the inevitable convergence of computer, Internet, and other mass media technologies, we can only imagine what's ahead.

Recent surveys document the phenomenal penetration that TV has in our daily lives. Some of the recent findings:

* Nearly 60 percent of children watch at least two hours of TV each day.

* Two out of three children surveyed live in a home that has three or more TV sets.

* More than half of the children surveyed had a TV set in their bedroom.

* Roughly one-quarter of America's dinners are eaten while watching TV.

* Nearly 20 percent of survey respondents report that they could not survive without television.

* Four of every five adults in the United States reported that watching TV with their children is a "family activity."

Marshall McLuhan, the media visionary from Canada who actually coined the term "media," argued that Marconi's invention of the wireless telegraph in the late 1800s ushered in a totally new era of human history. It was, McLuhan argued, only the second time that the fundamental form of information transmission had radically changed. The first revolution took place with the invention of the printing press. McLuhan believed that print technology wiped out a culture based on tribal unity and the oral tradition of communication. Likewise, he thought that electronic technology would ultimately wipe out a culture based almost exclusively on print communication. McLuhan did not believe that the content of the media was nearly as important as many of us fear. What mattered, he thought, was the huge effect of the media *per se.* He thought that human beings would find electronic media to be inherently involving and almost impossible to avoid.

The statistics tend to support McLuhan. Yet, while they still turn on the tube, people express concern about how popular culture has degenerated as a result of the media, particularly the effects of violence and sex on society and (especially) on children (and remember that one-half of the children in the above-mentioned survey had televisions in their bedrooms!). Many people suspect that the violence in media has caused an increase in crime and violence in society, and that sex in media has caused a deterioration of our collective morality. Such worries seem reasonable and plausible.

Scholars have, of course, studied the effects of media for decades. Back in the late 1920s, a privately funded research project, the Payne Fund Studies, set out to explore the effects of movies on young people. These studies dealt with the content of movies (primarily romance and sexuality) and how movies affected children's learning, attitudes, and moral values—even how children slept at night. These studies really initiated the "media effects" research tradition. The Payne Fund Studies were followed up by sporadic investigations of the effects of comic books and radio programs. In 1938, Orson Welles' radio drama, *The War of the Worlds,* actually triggered public panic, crossing a boundary between fictitious effects and realism.

Starting in the 1960s, with the explosion of television programming, newspapers started to carry stories of young children who had committed crimes that were, by their own admission, inspired by things they had seen on TV. The controversy about the effects of media violence on aggressive behavior has raged ever since. Over the last thirty years, violence and sex have dominated the research agenda of media scholars and much of the public debate about media effects. After more than forty years of scientific research on media effects, there is now a strong consensus that violence, sex, and horror definitely exert an influence on viewers. In August 2000, the American Medical Association and the American Psychiatric Association declared that violence in media does, indeed, have harmful effects on people and on children, in particular. But despite such assertions and our own intuition and gut suspicions, the documented effects of the media seem, in fact, to be quite modest.

Any reasonable, stable, law-abiding citizen knows that the violence they watched throughout their childhood has not ruined their lives. For instance, as a young and impressionable kid, I watched *The Three Stooges* almost every afternoon after school. I had a regular, daily dose of Stooge violence, including slaps, eye pokes, hammer blows, and hair ripping. But even as a seven-year-old, my reality testing was such that I knew the difference between imitating violent antics and causing real physical injury. I never had an impulse to run a saw down my brother's head or slap him across the face. While my friends and I would hold out our hands and say, "Pick two fingers" like Moe, we would only fake poking someone in the eye.

Most of us would probably say the same, "I have watched many shootings, beatings, and murders. It would never occur to me to commit an act of violence. I respect the rights of others." And conversely, we know there are people who do not watch media violence and yet become aggressive and violent. Most aggressive behavior cannot be explained by the amount of media violence a person watches. The effect probably doesn't exceed 10 percent. This means that roughly 90 percent of the aggression or lack of aggression has to be explained by other factors. We can speculate about what the other factors might be. They might include genetic predisposition to violence, personal anger and frustration in one's life, and the values and behavior taught in the home.

The findings for media violence are pretty typical for nearly any media effect that is studied by researchers. Exposure to sexually explicit images might account for roughly 10 percent of the variation in attitude changes toward sex, family values, and the like. Exposure to frightening films may account for roughly 10 percent of the variance in the experience of sleep disturbances and nightmares. The bottom line is that it is rare to be able to account for much more than 10 percent of any given human behavior by appealing to media content.

It would be so much simpler if we could document a direct association between television and film content and social and antisocial behavior. We would then know what action to take. But it isn't this simple. Twelve-year-olds imitating stunts from professional wrestling can get seriously injured. But it doesn't mean that all of them who watch will grow up to become antisocial brawlers.

It's Not What's On

The intense focus on media content means that we've spent little time or energy investigating McLuhan's prime thesis: that the *presence* of electronic media, regardless of content, has a profound effect on us. If, instead, we consider the effects of the media in terms of personal isolation, we might be able to put our worries about violence and sex into a more useful context. The social problem created by television and other electronic media are their very existence and the way they dominate our lives. Cut off as we are from our natural sources of intimacy, we turn to media instead of other people to cope. We spend hours upon hours looking at screens instead of into faces. Are we doing this because we are too alone? Or are we so alone because we spend too many hours looking at screens? It could be both. By choosing to devote so much of our life to the passive distractions of media, we have isolated ourselves from others. And, in turn, this compensates for the isolation we have unwittingly created by our mobility and our independent lifestyles characterized by striving for success. It is little wonder that the cover story of a recent *Scientific American* featured the problem of television addiction.

Is there any other support for this idea that television's more important impact is its isolating effects? One research project on media effects reported some startling statistics. Brandon Centerwall, a University of Washington researcher, presented an exhaustive analysis that showed that the homicide rate in the United States doubled after the introduction of television. The same thing happened in South Africa. The statistical analysis is careful and compelling. After reading his study, it really does appear that increasing homicide is one of the effects of TV that we have to entertain seriously. But why should this correlation emerge? The standard interpretation indicts the violent *content* on TV as the major culprit. This seems like a reasonable assumption because we do know from experimental evidence that exposure to violent images does increase aggressive behavior. However, the magnitude of the effect he found appears to be much larger than the content effects that come out of experimental research (remember the 10 percent figure?).

So could Centerwall's data lead to another conclusion? Perhaps this increase in homicides has less to do with any particular kind of content that viewers watch on TV, and more to do with the isolating and disconnecting effects of TV on our interpersonal relationships. Social research is clear: Loneliness and social detachment are more strongly associated with mental health problems than are any messages coming across in television or film. Disconnection and emotional isolation can lead to increased anger and frustration and are strongly correlated with aggressive interpersonal behavior. This sense of disconnection leads to incivility and aggression toward others whom we do not know. Even when violence occurs between family members, the barrier against our acting out aggressive impulses is clearly lowered more by a sense of isolation than by media depictions of violence. TV disconnects us from others, and this leads to a range of problems in larger society. As one researcher, Kathy Dobie, noted grimly:

> This year's hate killers are weak, lonely, Caucasian men who murder those who have what they don't: a sense of belonging. I haven't heard of anyone who spoke to Benjamin Smith during his three-day killing spree that ended in his suicide. As far as I know, he didn't pick up the phone late at night between killings and say goodbye to Mom or Dad. He didn't call his ex-girlfriend and say, "It's all your fault" or "I'm sorry" or something cryptic, a line from a song, perhaps, that we could've milked for meaning later. Like the high school killers in Littleton, Colo., Smith went after anyone who believed—in God, in family, in the rightness of their own existence—and anyone who belonged.

In his book, *The Sound Bite Society,* Jeffrey Scheuer argues that the convergence of media technologies "may also further isolate the rest of us, to the detriment of community and democratic life . . . perhaps more Americans will shutter themselves indoors to watch TV, avoiding social intercourse. There may be more me, less we." Scheuer also notes that the mass media may promote a trend toward social fragmentation. More and more people are carrying on virtual relationships that seem divorced from a physical reality. Internet researchers have already warned us about the possibility that overreliance on this new medium produces greater social isolation.

Emotional Involvement with Media Characters

Having left our families and having few connected relationships, we long for the experiences of emotional closeness. Into this void come *West Wing* and *Everybody Loves Raymond* to provide us with some of the sights, sounds, and feelings of friends and family. We come to know the characters and the issues they discuss; we feel like "insiders." The same might also be said for the popular shows of any era, from *Seinfeld* and *Friends* through *Ally McBeal, The X Files,* or the current crop of music television videos on-air personalities, even Ozzy Osbourne. All of them invite us to know and care about the characters as if we are in a real relationship with them. And not coincidentally, within these shows the characters frequently share emotional closeness and refrigerator rights with each other. Curiously, instead of acting on our own desire for deeper connections to others, the media age allows us to invest hours watching these connections played out fictitiously and two-dimensionally on television. It is no small irony that many of us could more accurately describe the kitchens of sitcom characters than the kitchens of our neighbors.

One line of study in mass communication has documented what scholars refer to as the "parasocial" relationship, a term describing the relationships we form with media characters and personalities. Studies tell us that such relationships are often highly charged with real emotion. Spending time with them may give us the *feeling* that we are part of the intimate connection—even though we are really on the outside looking in. Our emotional connection to media characters and personalities often becomes so intense that they actually feel quite real to us. Viewers even feel as if they "know" the animated characters on *The Simpsons.*

Research with college students suggests that their involvement with soap opera characters can start to resemble relationships with real people. The students become so engaged, they can predict how a show's characters will respond when dealing with different situations. They can analyze and articulate the attitudes they believe the characters will express in various circumstances. Dr. Cheri Sparks, Glenn's wife, is both a long-time TV soap fan and a social psychologist who has studied fans' reactions to soap characters. She writes:

> I have watched television soap operas since I was in high school. I am not particularly proud of this habit. But especially as a young mother and graduate student, while babies were napping, floors needed washing, or dissertation data were being entered, I would watch soaps. One day, I don't even remember exactly why, I happened on a website where people were talking about soaps. My first reaction to the idea of posting on a soap opera Internet board was one of scornful amusement. Who would spend time on the Internet talking about something as silly as a TV show, let alone a soap opera? But then, when I stumbled upon an Internet discussion about whether Luke really raped Laura or merely seduced her (*General Hospital*), I hesitated a long, thoughtful five seconds and then my fingers got tapping!
>
> Even ex-characters have a sort of life of their own—witness the website devoted to the character Todd Manning of *One Life to Live,* still going a year after the character had been written out of the soap. Not so surprising, perhaps, given the websites for J. R. Ewing, Rhett Butler, and Captain Kirk. But what *may* surprise you is that there exists heated debate regarding the *proper care and nurturing of a fictional character.* Todd was, at different times, a rapist, killer, liar, scam-artist, and general all-around bully. Yet, some online posters would regularly complain about any characters in the fictional town who were mean to Todd. They would offer defenses like, "The boy had such a bad childhood," and "Who wouldn't have a few problems if raised like he was?" Viewers posted long

descriptions of events that "probably" happened to Todd in his childhood, even though the character did not appear on screen until he was a young adult. Some viewers admitted that they were losing sleep worrying about what would happen to Todd.

You may not be watching soap operas yourself, but Americans as a group are spending an average of twenty-plus hours each week watching television. This means that we are all experiencing steady exposure to both real and fictitious characters. Although you may not watch any entertainment television, you have likely watched newscasters or sports commentators and, over time, feel as if you know them. It's comforting to see the familiar face of Peter Jennings or Katie Couric. This is unprecedented in human history.

What gets lost in all this, of course, is contact with real people. Connecting with media figures takes no effort on our part, unlike the hard work of building real-life relationships. The feelings of involvement and the "sounds of intimacy" that the media provide substitute for the real connection and intimacy we've lost through geographic relocation and separation from close friends over the years. Worse still, we pick up the taste for closeness through our relationships with media "friends"—but they can't be there for us when we need them. Jerry, Elaine, George, and Kramer won't be at the table for Thanksgiving dinner. The media have, perhaps, served up an easier and more accessible source of connection to people living in a culture that is relationship-starved. We reach out through the television and computer screen—even the disembodied voices coming across the radio speakers.

Talk Radio:
The Sounds of Lost Intimacy

Many predicted that, as television became widespread, it would supplant and eventually kill off radio as a popular medium. Radio did, indeed, go through some major changes, but it is far from dead. When we can't watch TV—say, while we're driving or at work— the radio keeps us tuned in and connected. Over a decade ago, two communication researchers recognized that talk radio was functioning not so much as *mass* communication, but as *interpersonal* communication. People find talk radio relaxing, exciting, and entertaining. It passes the time and provides companionship. Does this sound like how we might describe our own close relationships? As we have become increasingly mobile and individualistic, radio has become another substitute for the gratification that person-to-person relationships typically provide.

In an article titled, "Talk Radio: The Private-Public Catharsis," the author noted that both callers and listeners in the talk-radio audience apparently have their needs for interpersonal communication partially met by the experience of the radio talk show. In essence, talk radio gives the illusion that we're having an intimate chat with close friends. On many morning drive-time radio programs, the conversation includes laughter and shared stories and observations, as well as disagreement, debate, and even personal attack. The talk vacillates between the lofty and the low, from topics of depth to the trivial. The tone moves from warm and friendly to mean-spirited in an instant.

Nationally syndicated programs such as *ESPN Sports Radio, Bob and Tom,* and *Howard Stern* all feature strong personalities and often include several cast members who share the microphone. Once you're used to the rhythm of the show, you feel as though you're one of the "inside group" sitting in the studio. When Dr. Laura

Schlessinger scolds her advice-seeking callers, it's like listening to a strong-minded mother or aunt dressing down a nitwit cousin. We forget that she has never met her callers and she never will. We are taken with our felt connection to her as if we know her. It creates the feeling of interaction. Even when calling into a radio program to vent feelings and opinions, we are doing so anonymously. It is not the kind of expression that leads to relationship building.

Real family conversation may have boundaries, but it does not strictly abide by larger cultural norms. It is not politically correct. So, too, with talk radio. Before long and without being aware of it, listeners feel a sense of familiarity as these programs take on the sounds of a family conversation, complete with ridicule, petty squabbles, and shared pleasures. New boundaries are created, and regular listeners soon learn them. It is no surprise that the two time periods of the radio broadcast day that have by far the largest listening audience are morning and afternoon drive time, when people are alone in their cars. Joseph Dominick, a mass communication scholar, echoes our theme. He states:

> Radio keeps people company in their cars. People who might otherwise be deprived of social relationships find companionship in media content and media personalities. In fact, some go so far as to develop feelings of kinship and friendship with media characters. Audience members might react to media performers and the characters they portray as if the performers were actual friends.

If intimate relationships are necessary for healthy living, could it be that as our relationships diminish in contemporary culture, we are drawn to the mass media to give us a taste of the nuances of our lost intimacy? As we listen to talk shows, we are at least hearing the *sounds* of intimate communication.

The Internet:
The End of Passive Media

Just as radio gave way to TV in the 1950s, so it now looks as though both television and radio are giving way to the digital era. We may look back to the dawn of the twenty-first century as the beginning of a new phase in the electronic revolution. Computer and Internet communication are increasing at an astounding pace. According to the most recent data, nearly 9 percent of the world's population is online now. This may seem like a very small number, until you remember that less than 1 percent was online only four years ago. We are in the midst of a global communication revolution. If you are reading this even a few months after publication, these data are already far too old. In the United States, online users are increasing at a rate of more than ten million per month. The United States currently has about 165 million Internet users, leading the world. Japan is a distant second at about fifty million users.

Some enthusiasts hope that the Internet might offer an antidote to the problems of isolation—that it's a step up from such passive forms of media as television, radio, and film. At least via the Internet, individuals are in reciprocal, interactive contact and can create new relationships and communities. Most of us who regularly use e-mail and chat services know how expressive the interactions can be. We can even put keystrokes together to represent emotions—a smile, a frown, puzzlement, and tears. But these cyber-only relationships are relatively weak compared to face-to-face relationships maintained on a regular basis. And they pale into triviality compared to relationships with family and long-standing friends.

There are millions now active in the chat room culture that profess to feeling very emotionally close to their online friends. Several confessed that they feel more open and candid in these relationships than they do with the other people in their life. Stephen, for exam-

ple, lives in his hometown but told us his most important connections are now online:

> I haven't moved in fifteen years and feel pretty connected to my
> town and the people I work with every day. However, most of
> these people do not have a close enough relationship that they
> would have refrigerator rights in my home. In fact, there are very
> few people in my life right now who have those rights, outside of
> my immediate family. Curiously, I have met many people through
> online chat rooms and have developed a very strong bond with
> them over the course of the last two years. Ironically, I feel close
> enough that I would consider them to have such rights if they ever
> came to my house. Although since we have never met in the flesh,
> maybe I'm just dreaming. But the truth is that I feel emotionally
> closer to the friends I have developed online than many of the
> casual friends who are all around me. I'm not sure what that says
> about me or this new "cyber-society" we have created.

What it says, among other things, is that it's easier to begin
the process of becoming emotionally connected through the anonymity of the Internet than to kick off a deeper relationship with
the person next door or at the next desk. In one recent survey, researchers at Carnegie Mellon University studied the impact on
emotional health of communicating over the Internet. They found
that some people could sustain "strong ties" over the Internet, but
that these were family and close friends with whom they already
share an intimate connection. Among those who create ties online,
they typically were described as "weak ties." Most interesting was a
kind of relationship paradox suggested by the authors. It seems that
many people might turn to the Internet as a way of trying to increase interpersonal connection, but these relationships, while engaging, typically remain weak ties. And here again, like the caller to

the radio station, we maintain a level of anonymity. While this may be appealing, it is doing nothing to further the relationships we need. Healthy relationships demand a higher level of mutuality, responsibility, commitment, and accountability. We shouldn't be surprised that the Internet pornography business is booming. Many spouses have testified to the obsession with the Internet for the evocative stimulation that people are missing in real life. Anonymity is the seductive lure of the modern media age.

Sadly, the time that is invested in forging these connections could be better used in forming stronger and more lasting relationships with others who are physically nearby and accessible. It's a curious phenomenon that those we interviewed who were most optimistic about the Internet and impassioned about its potential to forge connections with others were themselves devoting hours online in lieu of investing in the relationships available all around them. There seemed to be a tacit bias that cyber-connections were preferable to physically proximate connections, regardless of evidence to the contrary.

Of course the Internet has been a life-enhancing development for people who are isolated for whatever reason. The homebound, the chronically ill, and those living in remote areas have found the Internet, e-mail, and instant chat a life-changing experience. Sally and I spoke at a state education conference in Alaska, which included teachers from all the districts throughout that amazing state. Most work in geographically remote areas in conditions of severe isolation. (Not surprisingly, depression and suicide are major problems for the schools and communities there.) For these professionals, access to the resources and relationships available on the Internet has been a real boon. But this is surely the exception to the rule. Most concentrated Internet use is by individuals who are not physically remote from other people.

Human beings will never be able to change a simple rule of relationships that the authors of the Internet study observed: "Generally, strong personal ties are supported by physical proximity." The kind of interdependence, commitment, and intimacy that serve to buffer you from the stresses of your life are most easily fostered by relationships that occur when you are in the direct physical presence of the other. Cheri Sparks, our resident social psychologist, reflected on the fragility of Internet relationships that form around the fictional relationships of soap opera characters:

> Internet friendships sprung up and then were lost over Todd, Tea, and Blaire, characters in *One Life to Live.* One raging debate concerned whether Todd's former wife Blaire or his former wife Tea was better for him. Feelings related to these issues erupted into such ugliness that websites went online as "safe havens" for fans of Todd and Tea. . . . In the same way that my relationship with a neighbor might be damaged if she were to vociferously defend someone who hurt my close friend, Internet relationships were destroyed because of feelings that began with loyalties regarding a fictional couple.

The issue raised in such anecdotes is the significance of physical presence for deepening emotional ties with another person. While we become emotionally involved watching television and film, its expression is contained and remains private.

We engage media in a very different manner than we do our interpersonal relationships. Sitting still and gawking at the screen for hours at a time, it's a wonder we retain any ability to communicate in person with each other. For instance, because we use visual clues all the time in interpersonal communication, I sometimes wonder if we might not be losing our skill at face-to-face interaction as a result of a media culture. We might have unwittingly created a society of starers and gapers. Our participation in conversation with another relies on giving and receiving visual clues about how we are being heard. If I tell you about something that happened to me and I'm very excited about it, my body language and facial expression will convey my enthusiasm. Without having to say it, I fully expect that you are going to react with reciprocal emotions that tell me you are sharing my experience. But even if television viewing does not atrophy interpersonal skills, it does draw us into the fascination of looking and being gripped by the spectacle. When visiting my grandsons, I usually have to shout or stand in front of them to block their view and divert attention from the television. "Dinner time!" They only hear me when they see me.

If you calculate the hours spent in fixated fascination to amazing visual images on the screen, we lose a staggering amount of time to idle absorption with minimal reward. How many hours have I lost by just staring at a screen? More importantly, what have I missed developmentally in my ability to effectively communicate with others? After the dubious opportunity to witness millions of fascinating events in the media, events far more riveting than I am likely to encounter in real life, what has happened to my capacity for enthusiasm in simple human discourse? I will always remember the cartoon that showed a father and son staring with delight at a beautiful sunset on the television screen, oblivious to the exact same scene in real life outside the adjacent window.

Television Instead of People

Given the current habits of relocating away from family at an unparalleled rate, it is not surprising that the amount of time we spend paying attention to *media* images of people instead of to *real* people is higher than ever before. Our culture of social separation shifts the balance between real human contact and media substitutes for human contact. It becomes a sick cycle. We move away and lose our key relationships. We cope by using television, radio, and the Internet to fill the void. And these media habits, in turn, become an impediment to reconnecting with real people. The media don't start the problem, mobility does. But the media present an unwitting yet overwhelming obstacle to remedying the isolation our moving around has caused us. Taken together, geographical relocation—coupled with our desire for independent success—and the rise of electronic media represent huge forces that have had much to do with the tendency for our drifting away from each other. If this is true, then the media are not perpetrators as much as accomplices to the problems of a separated society.

The idea that we may be using the media to replace relationships with real people is supported by current research in mass communication. The title of Byron Reeves' and Clifford Nass' recent book, *The Media Equation—How People Treat Computers, Television, and New Media Like Real People and Places,* reflects this new reality. According to the authors, the attraction of moving images is rooted in brain activity: "Motion in *pictures,* especially motion that appears directed at the viewer, stimulates physical activation in the brain as if the moving objects were actually present." They summarize their major thesis about media by stating:

> Media experiences equal human experiences . . . there are few discounts for media, few special ways of thinking or feeling that are unique to media, and there is no switch in the brain that is activated when media are present. People's responses show that media are more than just tools. Media are treated politely, they can invade our body space, they can have personalities that match our own, they can be a teammate, and they can elicit gender stereotypes. Media can evoke emotional responses, demand attention, threaten us, influence memories, and change ideas of what is natural. Media are full participants in our social and natural world.

We believe that Reeves and Nass provide some insight as to *why* people find media to be so compelling and tend to use it as a substitute for *in-the-flesh* relationships. The people who appear in entertainment media feel, in many ways, like real people to us. And they are available at a flick of a switch. We can invite them into our living rooms in an instant and kick them out just as quickly. Yet while they're present, we feel like we're getting something of the taste of real relationships. In one sense, NBC's *Friends* may seem more appealing than *your own* friends.

Glenn sometimes compares the media to a scratch-and-sniff sticker, where you open a magazine and see an ad that you scratch to smell the fragrance of a flower or salty air from the seashore. The aroma is an instrument to stimulate your memory about a past experience and prompt you to buy the product. Obviously, it isn't like the experience itself, but a pale comparison. In some ways, when media depictions draw us into a web of personalities, debates, and emotions, they are like a scratch-and-sniff experience. They resemble real-life intimacy and evoke feelings and memories of our most intimate connections. In itself, there's nothing wrong with this experience and it can be pleasant. But just as we might worry about the fool who *habitually* used substitute experiences for real-life experiences, we should also pity those of us who *habitually* substitute media relationships for real-life connections and the intimacy that can only be realized face to face.

Opting for time in front of a television or computer screen makes it all the more likely that you will not make the reconnections crucial to your well-being. This thesis does not just apply to those of us who relocate or those who have had loved ones move away. It applies to all of us. In a society that is simultaneously media saturated and interpersonally disconnected, the most pertinent concern is the role media are playing in our loss of refrigerator rights.

Points to Remember

❖ The social problem created by television and other electronic media are their very existence and the way they dominate our lives. Cut off as we are from our natural sources of intimacy, we turn to media instead of other people to cope. We spend hours upon hours looking at screens instead of into faces.

❖ While most of the cultural discussion about mass media revolves around the effects of particular types of content such as violence and sex, we ought to be worrying more about the simple effect of the presence of the media on our daily relationships.

❖ We habitually try to substitute various sorts of media for deep, interpersonal relationships. While the media provide some of the atmospherics of close relationships, they ultimately fail to provide the real thing.

What We Need

We Need to Recognize
Our Symptoms of Detachment

*Once again we conclude that the basic nature of humanity is
compassionate rather than aggressive, our relationship to the
world around us changes immediately. Seeing others as basically compassionate instead of hostile and selfish helps us relax, trust, and live at ease. It makes us happier.*

—DALAI LAMA, *The Art of Happiness*

Denying Detachment

Has someone ever suggested that you were "in denial" about something? In my younger years, when I was far less reflective, I was in
denial about a lot of matters, especially about such things as my impatience and my temper, for example. I came to this conclusion on
my own with the help of psychotherapy. Maybe someone had ac-
cused me of being in denial before that—I don't remember. I must
be in denial about this as well.

We hear the term *denial* a lot these days. Usually, it means that we
are not facing some emotionally charged issue in life. You might be
"in denial" about your drinking habits, the way you treat your
spouse, or your growing mountain of credit card debt. Maybe you
refuse to see reality, or maybe you're genuinely unable to see the
problem. It's amazing what tricks our minds can play on us when
the emotional stakes are high enough. And we don't like someone

telling us we are "in denial" even if deep down we suspect they are right.

Our culture is, we believe, in denial about our problem of inter-personal isolation. Instead of facing up to our need for more rela-tionships and deeper intimacy, we distract ourselves with other mental activities to help us pretend we're just fine. Our denial pre-vents us from recognizing that our isolation is driving many of our other life problems. Distracting activities help to compensate; they relieve us, at least temporarily, from symptoms of stress that actually derive from our disconnection.

Up to this point I have tried to make the case that we've lost re-frigerator rights because of geographic mobility, our quest for in-dependence, and the numbing distraction of mass media. I have included personal illustrations from my own life, as well as from Glenn's and others we have interviewed. And maybe you have fol-lowed along in general agreement with the observations but still don't sense its applicability to your own life. If you are like me, you have no trouble seeing how others are being affected but not your-self. Psychologists call this the "illusion of personal invulnerability." Others are vulnerable—but I'm not. We see the spot of dust in our brother's eye, but not the plank in our own. We deny. We rational-ize. We create illusions. But might it be that you, too, have under-estimated the profound effects of your own loneliness? Is it possible that some of what is bothering you may be caused or at least made worse by your loss of relationships?

If I have learned anything over the years of my own journey of angst and growth, it is the amazing ingenuity of the human mind to create defensive techniques that mask the foundations of our pres-ent fears and restless feelings. These strategies, although clever, keep us stuck where we are—floundering by our own wits to remake our attitude and feel better. In our strain to believe that we can get along without emotional intimacy, we use many different strategies. Here

I would like to talk about three that I find very common. We cope with aloneness through our belief that we can:

❖ Maintain personal control

❖ Find gratification and even happiness in material accumulation

❖ Feel better by staying busy

How do these beliefs relate to isolation? They may look at first like neutral or even positive approaches more than problems to be addressed. Let's consider each in turn.

1) Maintaining Personal Control

Loss of control is a great fear for each of us; perhaps it's *the essential* human fear. Feeling that we are no longer in control of what is happening to us is a fundamental threat to our well-being. It underlies almost every painful and terrifying experience we can have in life.

And it can hit with horrifying suddenness.

Your son has been in an accident!
I'm sorry, but the lump is malignant.
You're fired!

Some people can handle a crisis with surprising calm, but crumble as soon as the trauma subsides. But even if we manage to repress anxiety in the crunch, it still hits us hard in the long run.

We're thinking about phasing out your department.
Okay, your next chemotherapy treatment
will be in four weeks.
I'm sorry, but the promotion went to Jess.
You will be reporting to him now.

You have your own story to tell of times when the rug was pulled out from under your feet. This is the great challenge of living, although I have a sense that in today's social, political, and psychological climate, the uncertainties feel more terrifying to us now.

I recall being on vacation in Colonial Williamsburg, Virginia. Sally and I toured an old church, which had a cemetery attached. Wandering around the nineteenth-century tombs, we were struck by the number of babies and young children buried there. One family plot had small white markers for Sara (aged two), Samuel (four), and Mary (eight). The guide reminded us that only a century ago, when my own great-grandparents were alive, common ailments like flu or injuries from a simple broken bone could kill anyone. Young children were vulnerable to diseases such as diphtheria that we never have to think about today. How would we feel if one of our children died of a simple flu? We would be stunned; we would question our faith; in our outrage and anger, we would certainly sue the doctor. In our world, we expect to overcome, to conquer, to control.

Children still die every day, despite our high-powered technology and advanced medical care. But we no longer face life's fragility with our ancestors' stoic acceptance. Their expectations were lower than ours, because their circumstances were so much more precarious than ours. They couldn't assume, as we do, that their children would grow to adulthood and live long and prosperous lives. They had humbler expectations of a world full of harsh realities. Today, in contrast, we believe that science and technology can overcome all our challenges. We believe that sooner or later, we *will* find that cure for cancer. We're convinced that high-tech will make our lives simpler, easier, better—that we'll have more choices, more control.

Along with our ability to do and control more comes the expectation that we will be more productive. Nowhere is this more evident than in the modern workplace. Managers and employees are under relentless pressure to succeed and thrive. If profits aren't as high as they were last year, the stock could crash. As competition gets tougher and new technologies make forecasting dicey, the stakes are huge. Setting aggressive new goals elevates everyone's anxiety levels. A single misstep, a misreading of the market, a bad guess, or a good guess under the wrong circumstances—any of these could erode or erase the company's gains and market share. With the dawn of the high-tech era, we're not seeing an easing of tension, but instead, an intensification of it. The name of the game is to control the variables.

Composure under such pressure has become among the most revered qualities in the work environment, trumping raw intellectual acuity; it is on par with, or perhaps even surpasses, social skill as a valued human commodity. In both professional and personal life, losing control under stress significantly affects how you are perceived and rewarded. But we're not all created equally cool under pressure. For every individual with a Zen Master temperament, there are probably nine others of us who find the stress of slipping control acutely discomforting.

More than ever in history, we believe in rationality. We expect and depend upon the integrity of cause-and-effect thinking. "If I do these things, I will be successful." We seem less prepared than previous generations for the unforeseen, unexpected events. It's threatening to confront how alone and cut off we are, how vulnerable and close to being out of control we seem to be. Isn't it curious that even in our age of reason there has been a surge in popularity of telephone psychics and astrological forecasts? Even the simplest logic defeats their basic premise: If psychics really have powers to see the future, why aren't they all rich from gambling and winning state lotteries? Yet millions of us turn to these sources daily. The psychic phone lines make billions of dollars annually. Perhaps the popularity of the paranormal is being fed by an insatiable desire to gain control over life events. The desire is so strong that it overwhelms mere reason.

The messages we get, in everything from television entertainment and advertising to popular psychology and business success literature, put enormous emphasis on the individual. They are aimed at *my* personal desires and needs. This emphasis on the individual reinforces the notion that life is essentially a solitary endeavor. Others around me are also on their own as well. We've come to believe that our success or failure in life depends principally on our own efforts. Self-help books urge us to take control of our life. In the end, the illusion of personal control is rooted in a dubious exaggeration of our cultural value of personal independence.

It stands to reason that if you lack close ties to others, the only rational response is to live and cope alone. Our thought is essentially that because I share my life with fewer intimates, I make more of my personal decisions alone, with less input from others around me. More of what I do is not observed or monitored by anyone. I basically live by my own wits. This mind-set alters how we react to feedback from other people. If we come to trust and depend on our own judgment moment to moment, it changes how we filter input. We not only have to assess the evident wisdom of any advice they offer; we must also weigh it against our perception about their integrity and trustworthiness.

This is less so with close intimates. For instance, if your mother has always been a source of good advice, you hear her without having to stop and evaluate the soundness of her judgment. This is true to one or another degree with any of your close relationships— with all those who have refrigerator rights in your life. Each of us could reel off the names of family members and instantly evaluate the value of their advice in any given area. Your uncle Harry may be the last one on earth you would go to for relationship advice but the first one you would call if your car broke down. As for his wife, your aunt Barbara, the exact opposite may be true.

But what if you lack close friends and family? Who then can

advise you when you have important choices to make? Then you have to turn to experts—and sometimes the experts contradict each other. Or too often what they say runs counter to your own intuition about what's right for you in your situation. How do you know whom to trust? No wonder we increasingly come to rely on ourselves. But we alone decide what's best and are never completely sure that our decisions are the right ones. It's a high cost—the price we pay to be in command of our own lives—as if we could do that, really.

Studies over the past several decades have established that some of us have an *internal locus* of control, meaning that we believe that we direct the course of our lives from within ourselves. *I can make my reality and change my fate.* In contrast, others of us have an *external locus* of control; that is, we view the circumstances outside ourselves as the primary determinants of what will happen to us. *I am at the mercy of these forces and cannot expect to control much in my life.* Recent research in this area has indicated that the two styles react to change and uncertainty very differently. Those with an internal locus of control suffer uncertainty far more profoundly. A study in the *Journal of Counseling Psychology* stated that "persons with exaggerated notions of personal control or with considerable previous experience in controlling the important events in their lives find uncontrollable outcomes particularly stressful . . . [T]hese individuals often fail to recognize that such outcomes are beyond their control and waste considerable effort trying to alter uncontrollable situations."

The thesis has also garnered more recent support in the literature. One researcher who has devoted many years to the study of coping with stress, Herbert Lefcourt, has provided some corroboration of the basic idea. In his review, he reports that in dealing with stressful events that are clearly beyond one's control, *those who have a high internal locus of control only seem to cope well when they have strong social support. They need good friends.* Lefcourt noted one study that found that when mothers who had a high sense of personal mastery over life's circumstances had to face the stress of a child who became critically ill, *they coped best when they had strong social support or high intimacy with a close friend.*

The need for personal control arises especially when we're detached from our sources of strength, our intimate, dependable bonds. And worse, this illusion of personal control is antithetical to our emotional growth and well-being. We believe that the control fantasy is mostly a compensatory reaction to a life that is too individualistic and separated from others. When I have to cope with my responsibilities alone, without the support of others, my isolation digs deep into my sense of adequacy and security. Nobody will pick me up if I fall. In contrast, when I am attached to trusted others with whom I share these responsibilities, the burden never falls on me alone. When facing surgery without others nearby to care about and for me, I struggle with my fears and worries by myself. I can't even count on having someone drive me home from the hospital and look after me while I'm convalescing. I need people who will commiserate with me and care enough to allow me to share my experiences. And I also need people who care enough to look after me.

Relying on the self betrays our own disconnection and ultimately reflects a crisis of faith: *I need only believe in myself.* We need to share life's uncertainties with others if we hope to sustain our emotional equilibrium. Even in religious faith, the experience of believing is one that is shared with other people of faith. It is life *within a community* that makes faith operative and alleviates the burden of the individual and personal suffering. Even people of strong faith get cancer and lose their children in car wrecks. But the resource they have is a family of caring others who alter how they respond to life's treacheries. Others help you make different meaning about life's eventualities than you would make on your own. While religious believers might pray in solitude, they live shoulder-to-shoulder with others in their faith community. They find the spiritual power of the divine not only in solitary meditation, but in the company of pilgrims.

Whether you find connection through your family of origin or some other constructed gathering, shared reality is significantly more advantageous than solitary reality, given the certainty of life's unpredictability. Personal control is a very poor way of coping.

2) Seeking Happiness in Material Accumulation

Although seeking material gratification has always been part of the human experience, it seems that in modern culture we spend an enormous amount of our energy pursuing *things* to make us happy. Even at a subtle level, we seek tangible evidence of our achievements: a job promotion, a desired date, a positive review, the accomplishments of our children. I haven't been all that motivated to acquire cars or homes, but I've certainly gone after career success and achievement. Although I've not coveted my neighbor's wife or his stuff, I've obviously coveted status and respect. For instance, between us, Glenn and I have accumulated eight academic degrees. Good grief! But we're not alone here. Many focus intensely on striving and acquiring.

Few of us—even us achievement types—would ever be so foolish as to claim that material possessions are the true source of happiness and fulfillment. When asked to name what we value in life, no one is crass enough to say "my Mercedes" or "my vacation home." Most of us would prefer to say "my faith" or "my family" or "the importance of the work I do." But we rarely are asked such questions. Instead, we spend most of our time and energy in pursuing immediate and tangible goals. And typically, our success at reaching these goals is measured in concrete terms. The seeming disconnect between the higher values we espouse, on one hand, and the way we live our daily lives, on the other, is probably why both social scientists and casual observers notice that otherwise successful people often feel unfulfilled. Although hard to document, there seems to be a general sense of uneasiness, if not downright alienation, among many people, regardless of their state in life. Perhaps this is always the case. In every time and place, there are voices of discontent. But even if this is not unusual, it still makes sense to try to understand it, if we can. What are the sources of our discontent in the here and now? Why are we uncomfortable in the midst of so much plenty?

The essence of the modern lament is a chronic longing for *more*: more stuff, more happiness, more fulfillment. The burgeoning interest in psychological insight says much about our feelings of uneasiness and restlessness. It's curious that we have so much and yet it doesn't seem to be enough. It reminds me of the joke about the young polar bear who asks his father, "Dad, are we polar bears?" "Yes," the father responds. "Yeah, but are we *real* polar bears?" the son presses. "Absolutely," the father responds firmly. The next day the young bear persists, "Dad, is there any chance that one of our ancestors was something other than a polar bear?" The father is exasperated and says adamantly, "Look, I'm a pedigree polar bear, and so is your mother! Why do you keep asking?" The youngster says, "Well, Dad, because I'm freezing!" When by all appearances my life seems blessed, why am I not warmed by what I have to enjoy? Why are some of us freezing?

It may well be that underlying our emotional discomfort is a hunger for more (and more definite) meaning in our life. If this is so, the issue is as much spiritual as it is psychological. That's probably why we often seek help in both quarters. Many people spend two hours each week seeking help: one on a couch, the other in a pew. It would make things so much easier if we could just be certain we knew what was wrong. But a convincing diagnosis for our feelings of discontent is elusive.

I'm sure by now you could guess that Glenn and I believe that the problem here has to do with the loss of refrigerator rights, the absence of family and neighbors, and our emotional distance from other people. As we have already proposed, our natural tendency is to compensate for this loss in a variety of ways. In addition to becoming more self-reliant and dependent on personal control, we also tend to seek our meaning in material reward. Despite the shrill critique of some scolds and moralists, we don't believe we do this because of shallow character or moral degradation. We do it because possessions and achievements are a readily available and culturally approved source of self-affirmation and personal meaning. But it is relationships, not possessions, that affirm our personal value and give us a sense of meaning. The love and support of my intimates is far more persuasive and gratifying than any possession, however rich and important. But if there is no such presence nearby, I will find what I can where I can. It is only by default that I revel in my promotion, my Lexus, or my son's scholarship to college.

One media researcher has documented the link between materialism, desire, discontent, and advertising. Marsha Richins has argued that consumer desire definitely shapes the entire marketing and advertising industry. But advertising overfuels consumer desire and fosters dissatisfaction among viewers who simply don't have the means to acquire all the goods that commercials take for granted we should own. Most of us are savvy enough to realize that a commercial is merely a device suggesting a connection between their product and our happiness. I can distinguish between a media lure and a valid consumer motivation. But while advertising contributes to our culture of materialism, it also merely reflects our preexisting values. The question we need to answer is why are we so receptive to the lure of possessions? Smart people who know better than to believe that things bring lasting joy are, nonetheless, caught up in the fervor of accumulation. We know many good, well-meaning, civil people who are doggedly chasing material treats. But *why?*

One theory is that materialism is directly, yet subjectively, related to our quality of life. In an article that appeared in *Social Indicators Research,* Joseph Sirgy found that whether or not a person is satisfied with their present standard of living is a critical ingredient in determining their quality of life. But satisfaction with standard of living is not so much a function of any *objective* living standard. Instead, it is a function of how one perceives their present standard in comparison with an individually set goal. What this means is that materialistic people set goals for their standard of living that are highly unrealistic and even out of reach. Their goals tend to be set on the basis of their feelings, not their thoughts. They are apt to focus on ideals—what they deserve and what they think they need— instead of on what might be reasonable, based on past events and present abilities. As a result, materialists end up being perpetually dissatisfied with their standard of living, regardless of where it is relative to economic norms. Their goals are likely to be unrealistic and, thus, ensure a state of chronic frustration and disappointment. These findings certainly resonate with my life experience. I continually pursue my dreams, but my dreams become bigger and ever more elusive. My attitude makes it a dead certainty that I'll never arrive where I want to be, satisfied and at peace.

Two researchers found that students who were highly materialistic also tended to score higher on measures of envy and social anxiety than those who were less focused on possessions. The connection may have something to do with family relationships. A recent study found that young people who suffer from disrupted families adopt more materialistic attitudes than do young people who are raised in intact families. As the authors pointed out, young people from disrupted families may be thrust prematurely into a provider–consumer role. This new role may encourage the formation of materialistic values.

Another group of scholars observed that young people who experience feelings of insecurity that result from family disruption may attempt to assuage their insecurities by seeking control over objects or people. Such an attempt may result in materialistic thinking. One study concluded, "Our findings provide considerable evidence that family structure is related to both materialism and compulsive consumption." The authors of this study went on to note that "physical objects and acts of consumption can serve as important replacements for human contact." In other words, a materialistic attitude can be a ready compensation for missing relationships, especially close intimates. The negative psychological and spiritual effects of materialism have been well documented.

Some attribute our obsession with accumulation to flawed values. This is a recurring theme on news, talk television, and radio. We often hear about the "erosion of values" over the last few generations. Condemnation of the greed of the consumer culture has long been a staple of preaching both in pulpits and popular media. The preachers, lay or religious, assume that materialism is in opposition to "traditional values," which, according to their proponents, center life's meaning in faith, family, and duty to country. Some believe that the past few generations have failed to inculcate these ideals into their children's souls and psyches. The decent among us (so the argument goes) are being infiltrated by a growing cadre of the selfish and the self-serving who are obsessed with their own prosperity with no real regard for anyone around them. But we don't find this view persuasive at all. Rather, we attribute our obsession with things to a form of compensation for our lost relationships. In the absence of gratifying interpersonal connections, we seek our pleasures where we can find them—even if it's at the mall.

If our materialism is not the result of wholesale moral decay, then what has brought us to such a place where we are rightfully seen as grotesquely materialistic? Certainly many outsiders view our society as narcissistic and believe that we see ourselves as the center of the universe. And though we pay lip service to community and family, we still seem to focus less on our identity as part of a group and more on the first person singular. Even in those moments when I am most occupied with activities of giving and loving, are my thoughts still centered on my self? In essence, do I view myself as a *me* instead of part of an *us*? Perhaps I shy away from close relationships because I'm afraid I might have to give up too much of *me* to become part of an *us*. I become my nearest, dearest, most available person, and I look to myself for signs of affirmation that I can't seem to get from others. Myself alone is a very lonely place to be—so lonely that I keep pursuing rewards to make myself feel loved. Getting that new toy—the state-of-the-art laptop, the sports car, the extravagant dinner, the fine wine—feels like a small dollop of self-love, and self-love sometimes feels like all the love that's going around.

In a healthy life, you balance your pursuit of goals and achievement with a life of full relationships. One feeds the other. But in such a life, you keep in mind that your fundamental self-worth and meaning lie in the whole of your life, not merely in your accomplishments, salary, or material achievement. The dogged pursuit of material goods and success is, we believe, only a compensation for the lack of connections—again a poor attempt to fill a glaring void. But materialism may be both a cause and an effect of our lack of intimacy—a cause, because materialism dissuades us from drawing others into our lives and keeping what we have to ourselves. But it is also an effect, because we reach for things to fill in the void in our lives.

In isolation, my instincts mislead me: I take what looks to be the safer, more secure approach of trusting in material success for personal happiness. I may know better, but I act as though material possessions will bring me peace and fulfillment. I'm like the Apostle Paul: "I do not do what I want—but I do the very thing I hate." To correct this, I need to be in touch with a wide array of intimate others, connections that will, in fact, leave me feeling loved, loving, and fulfilled.

3) Staying Busy

Another common defense against our feelings of isolation has a profound impact on our daily life—busyness. Millions of us relate to the complaint that there are not enough hours in the day to do what we need or want. Our lives seem a collection of clashing priorities and conflicting responsibilities. We might think of this issue as the problem of *regulating our external stimulation*. Many of us have difficulty striking a balance between activity and relaxation: that is, our lives are either overstimulated or understimulated. How many of us have a lifestyle that is so busy, it keeps us from doing more of what we love doing best? Working parents miss having enough time with their kids. Family members have so many commitments that they never seem to find time to eat dinner together. Career obligations steal the time and energy we need to have a real, fulfilling social life. Psychologist David Johnson argues that we depend on human relationships like these to provide, "the essential competencies required to survive in our world, and for fun, excitement, comfort, love, personal confirmation, and fulfillment."

In a broad sense, human relationships provide us with all kinds of *external stimulation,* the very kind we have needed since the day we were born. Developmental psychologists argue that babies need external stimulation for complex cognitive development. (I've always believed that my brain works really well because I spent my first few years in a noisy walk-up apartment in Brooklyn.) The benefits of such stimulation have been shown in systematic research studies. The brain needs stimulation to grow and function properly. As human beings, our richest and healthiest stimulation is being in the presence of and engaged with others. Right from infancy, there seems to be a built-in bias for human stimulation. Studies show that infants prefer looking at human faces than at other objects in their environment. This preference might develop after birth, but there is some evidence that infants are born with it. The research findings strongly suggest that we are wired to thrive in close connection with others. In addition to providing us with basic nurturing needs of love and companionship, intimate contact with other human beings also provides a necessary level of external stimulation throughout our lives. When we lose the intimacy, we lose the stimulation. When we lose the stimulation, we seek ways to compensate.

It may well be that much of the current epidemic of sensation-seeking behavior represents a desire to replace lost stimulation. Perhaps our attraction to media stimulation, the highs of cocaine and ecstasy, gambling and lotteries, and scandals and sensationalism, stem from our unspoken sense of disconnection. We may be drawn to professional wrestling and movies packed with sex, violence, and horror to try to compensate for the lack of the sort of stimulation provided by a rich web of close relationships.

Starting with this fundamental notion, it's reasonable to believe that the extended-family model provides the right balance and variety of stimulation we need. Not only does a family provide relationships with siblings and parents, it also includes grandparents, cousins, aunts, uncles, nieces, and nephews. It provides us with a network of relationships that crosses generations. We function best when we are embedded in this network of intimacy, because it provides the rich external stimulation we need.

Now, we use the phrase *rich stimulation* cautiously. Of course, family interactions are full of as much acid as honey. Family life is often as tense as it is comforting, and the compromises demanded can drive you nuts. There are times you want to scream and run from the very people who you know you love. But the mix of the warmth and the chill, the bile and the sugar is the very source of stimulation that gives us a full life. The tensions are mingled with the joys and give meaning and wholeness to a life. A life that divides our joys and our tensions into separate compartments strips each of their power and meaning. If your family is only about the tension and your friendships are only about the joy, your life is out of balance. The cheer of "good times only" friendships is too shallow, and the grief of isolation is too deep.

In the absence of close relationships, it stands to reason that we will try to compensate for what we're lacking by seeking suitable replacements. Our search for substitute stimulation arises out of the emotional vacuum created by our social separation. And in this vacuum we try to stay busy to fill the void. According to conventional wisdom, modern culture moves at a frantic pace. Trying to "keep up" (this view says) forces us to be so hyper-focused, busy, and exhausted that we lack the time or the energy for relationships with others. This view is now so prevalent that nobody questions it. You may be surprised, therefore, to learn that the average American actually has *more* leisure time today than thirty years ago. John Robinson's recent book, *Time for Life: The Surprising Ways Americans Use Their Time,* reports that Americans, "have almost five hours of free time more a week than they did in the 1960s."

Our initial reaction to Robinson's finding is skepticism or even downright disbelief. It doesn't jibe with most anecdotal observations about the way most people and families live their lives. We all complain that there aren't enough hours in the day even for the bare necessities. Our average weekdays seem to be a frenetic whirl of getting to work, shuttling kids, struggling to keep up with the housework, and trying to fit in at least a little family quality time. Many social observers identified the "fast pace of life" as a major contributor to stress and anxiety. Articles abound in health newsletters, media reports, and Internet postings bemoaning the stress caused by the fast pace of life. Recommended solutions also abound and range from increasing physical exercise to changing one's diet—even chiropractic and acupuncture. One college president was so impressed with the problems of the stress-filled, fast-paced life in America that he decided to write an entire book urging people to adopt "the simple life." In it he seemed to propose that if we want to reduce our stress, we should leave our urban environments and move to the woods. And he was *serious.*

How do we square the competing notions that we feel so pressed for time and yet we are working less hours than at any time in history? Hard as it might be to accept, perhaps the problem really lies in what we believe about the quality of our life—that is, the issue is more about perception than about time. Is there a difference between being overwhelmed and just *feeling* overwhelmed? Is there a difference between not really having enough hours and feeling swamped by our obligations? Is the problem time management or unrealistic expectations? How much of the blame can be put on external pressures? In contrast, *how much of what stresses us is self-imposed?* How do we disentangle the elements of our wild lifestyle?

Anyone who has been in psychotherapy soon becomes familiar with the idea that our own seemingly baffling behavior actually has an underlying logic. When I act in self-defeating ways, the therapist is trained to discover my real motivation. It's based on the assumption that I must be gaining something from my behavior that is more psychologically significant than what I am losing. For instance, anyone who is married and travels a lot knows that you must choose to be faithful while you're out on your own. It's not a complicated choice, but people devise their own approach for coping with the loneliness of the road. Some, of course, are thrilled to be off and running and have wobbly vows and dual lives that they juggle. But most find some way to be good soldiers and function while apart. My strategy was to become obsessively focused on my work. I scrupulously avoided circumstances of temptation so as not to become vulnerable to a fling or a road affair. I became so good at this that I had trouble deprogramming myself for reentry. I would come home and have a hard time reconnecting with Sally because I was still wearing my "shield-of-death loyal husband" emotional road armor. I was not consciously aware of this at first. We only noticed that I was irritable and curt in my interactions with her when I initially came home. This irritation was a self-defeating behavior because it denied me the contact I was deprived of while traveling. It was an inane yet effective strategy for marital faithfulness. And it had a logical explanation in that it was a way of upholding my commitments to my marriage. There was an underlying logic to my maladaptive behavior.

Using this idea, one possible explanation for the frenzied lifestyle we create is that we derive some beneficial stimulation that comes from the feeling of being so busy. And we may not be so eager to back away from this lifestyle too quickly because we instinctively know that without a wide array of close relationships at our disposal, we would immediately begin to suffer the ill effects of our losses. In other words, we might experience the depression that emerges from our *under*stimulation. In effect, this means that we might be filling our nonwork hours with activities and obligations that feel like work. We pursue our alleged recreation and so-called "down time" with the same focused vigor that we apply to our career. We feel like we are always working because we *are* always working. Using our leisure time to take on more responsibilities creates a real sense of accountability and commitment. But in truth, much of it is self-imposed. Combine this with the increased hours we spend watching television or playing on the computer, and the amount of time that *feels* available is further diminished.

Modern families often live by a rigid schedule that structures almost every available hour of time for themselves and their children. Recreation is as tightly timed as work and school. We have come to believe that, for healthy development, children need organized activities filling virtually all their time. We're obsessed with equipping our kids with skills—an obsession that misses the point. No matter how hard we push them to perform, they may not have the necessary talent. And even if your child is destined to have a career in sports or the arts, interactive play with others is more important developmentally than their dance, soccer, or violin lessons.

There was a time not long ago when most children played with each other for hours, with far less adult supervision than they often get today. Spending time with your children should feel more like leisure than work. But when we're strangers in our own neighborhoods and disconnected from extended family, we both turn *to* our kids and turn *on* our kids. We hyper-engage, hyper-parent, and enwrap, sometimes hovering and even smothering. And we lose hours and years to a sense of obligation and stressful attentiveness. It's stimulation, all right, but not in a way that builds any of us up.

All of us desire to be loving spouses and responsible parents. We also want to be committed to and emotionally energized by our careers. But we often feel that both parts of our life are suffering. Among those who are family-focused but compelled to work in order to make ends meet, pressures come from all sides, forcing undesirable sacrifices. *If I spend too much time concentrating on my job, my kids and marriage will suffer. But if I focus all my attention on my family, my career aspirations will never be fulfilled.* It seems that many of us are struggling with a balancing act to avoid slipping too far in either direction. Making matters worse, few feel free to talk about the tension, because admitting to either excess is politically incorrect. Each side has demanding voices. In one ear you hear your employer calling you to go the extra mile and meet your objectives for the good of the team. And in the other ear are the voices of your spouse, children, parents, and pastor challenging you about your priorities. No wonder we experience so much anxiety, guilt, and disappointment.

Day to day, we operate on a wing and a prayer, hoping that everything will fall into place, key tasks will get done, and there won't be any scheduling disasters. Predictably, however, there are sticks in the spokes of our spinning wheels. We are not stupid. We acknowledge that our frenetic lifestyle consigns all dimensions of life to the edges and everything we do is given short shrift. But we carry on somehow, usually with an unplanned, improvised rhythm, greasing whatever wheel is squeaking loudest this week. We've spent the last week absorbed by a work crisis. Now the kids are fighting more; they clearly need some undivided attention. So we turn our attention to them, trying to ignore the incessant demands of the job. We feel that we're spending all our time trying to plug the holes in the dike—that we can never really relax, because there's always something that needs our attention.

Stress in modern life has become synonymous with the sheer demands on our time. Is it really necessary for you to live this way? A frenzied lifestyle is, in the end, a poor substitute for the more meaningful close connection with others. Have we become so accustomed to the modern pace of life and the stimulation it provides that we can't even imagine life being any other way? The prospect of actually *stopping* this frantic running around might actually terrify some of us. And why not? The alternative is an absence of stimulation, and that might actually be a recipe for depression.

It seems to us no accident that at the same time we complain about our frantic lives, we are facing a near epidemic of depressive mood disorders. At least some of this phenomenon may be rooted in the loss of stimulation that is characteristic of isolation.

Sources of Energy

We know that the body computer is *not* in the sleep mode. We do everything we can to keep the body going at full steam. However, contrary to some of the wisdom *du jour,* our emotional energy does not come principally from engaging in personally enjoyable, solitary activities. Nor will energy come from diet, exercise, acupuncturists, aromatherapy, or vitamins alone. Lasting energy comes from a life in which we manage our challenges and worries with equanimity. And this perspective does not usually evolve out of thin air. It is achieved primarily through close, supportive interaction with those who help us find it. If I am anchored in such relationships, attending to my personal needs through healthy activity will sustain me emotionally, psychologically, and physically.

My refrigerator rights relationships give me feedback, help shape my perspective, and, thereby, adjust my mood. They help me manage my very busy life by feeding back perspective and, with that, my sense of being harried begins to wane. Only my intimates can credibly confront me about altering my self-destructive and troublesome behavior. And only intimates can do this while simultaneously affirming me in the most profound manner. Without such influences, left to my own resources, it is no surprise that I struggle to regulate my life's tempo in a wide variety of stimulating activities—activities that pale in comparison to the experience of knowing and caring for other human beings.

Points to Remember

❖ We live in denial of our social isolation. Because of our strong sense of independence, our natural urge is to adopt the belief that we control our own destiny and can "go it alone." In fact, we can't. We need each other.

❖ We like to deceive ourselves with the belief that our deepest impulses can be satisfied by accumulating material wealth. This is just another sign of our denial of our real need: refrigerator rights relationships.

❖ Relationships provide us with essential stimulation that we need for life. When we lack those relationships, we turn to other things to fill the void. The chronic levels of busyness that characterize our modern lives may, in fact, be the results of our attempts to substitute what's really missing—intimate connections with other people.

We Need Emotional Closeness

Human relationships are meant to be like two hands folded together. They can move away from each other while still touching with the fingertips. They can create space between themselves, a little tent, a home, a safe place to be.

—HENRI NOUWEN, theologian, *Bread for the Journey*

The Cultural Drift

Because our natural human inclination *is* to connect with and be emotionally close to other people, our culture is now in dire straits. The drift into individualism and isolation has now become so obvious that (at least to sociologists) American culture is unique. We are alone in the world in putting such heavy emphasis on individual versus group identity. Ours is a culture of fierce, personal independence. We take pride in individual competition, mastery, and achievement. We pay a steep price, however, as ours is also a culture of intense anxiety and psychic distress. As proud as we are of our way of life, there are aspects of other cultures worthy of envy— even those that lack our overblown material luxury.

An important theme in the sociological literature is the differences between "individualistic" and "collectivist" cultures. In collectivist cultures, people emphasize their dependence on each other, and family members work together harmoniously and cooperatively toward common goals. For example, right here in the midst of our society are thriving Amish communities that embody collective support and strong community. Close relations, social support, and cooperation are essential for family survival. Much like the America of a bygone era, these societies are often agrarian. The work on the farm requires the entire family, which also depends on a network of nearby families and neighbors, who face similar problems and opportunities and share common approaches and values. The individual matters, of course, but the central concern is for the harmony and well-being of the community.

By contrast, urban, industrialized, Western societies like ours are based on individual autonomy and personal fulfillment. We get very touchy when someone suggests that we are not independent, not "our own person." We value autonomy, self-reliance, freedom of choice and expression, personal achievement, and emotional independence. The individual's rights "trump" community cohesion. On the fringe of society there are paramilitary and religious extremist groups or cults that demand devotion to the group leader at all costs—even your own life. But these only serve to illustrate for the rest of us the danger of becoming engulfed in a group that can rob us of our precious individual identity.

For fifty years, we have been moving away from group and community norms and values to the norms and values of a mobile, individualistic, "techno-culture." Of course this shift has its pros and cons. And it's the costs that Glenn and I want to examine. As our emphasis on the individual becomes stronger, one of the losses we experience is a fundamental source of psychological and physical energy: emotional closeness, interdependence, and mutual care. Our patterns of mobility and technological lifestyle complicate this loss and move us ever further away from even minimal interdependence.

I have no real expectation that our social character will change

anytime soon. And I for one don't want to lose my personal independence or become swallowed up by my relationships and lose my
individual identity. I doubt that most of us are ready or willing to
surrender our aspirations for personal achievement. My life ambition and strong need for self-fulfillment are too much a part of
my identity to be jettisoned. But what do I do with this stress level
that comes along with my fierce individuality? Is there a balance to
be had?

The answer is not to fantasize that we can make a radical course
correction or hope to return to some nineteenth-century collec-
tivism. Although those cultures have their advantages, so do individualistic cultures. We don't want to lose what we've gained—but
we need to regain what we've lost. Individuality blunts the process
of friendship, while privatization short-circuits our potential for social support and connection to a larger group purpose. The afflic-
tion in our culture is that we seem to reject the very things that we
need. Instead of developing positive interpersonal relationships, we
develop habits that foster anxiety, depression, and alienation from
others. In this chapter, I want to identify some of our most basic
needs that contemporary culture increasingly fails to meet. Although
these needs might not seem particularly surprising to you, I'm betting that you've rarely thought about them in the context of the
cultural drift that has been discussed thus far.

Wired for Connection

Whether you're struggling with financial woes in Atlanta or lazing
in luxury in Chicago, running in exhausting circles in Los Angeles
or hanging in there as a single parent in Philadelphia, some things
never change. We humans have a few things in common. Every one
of us will flourish or perish depending on whether we have two ba-

sic things: physical and emotional sustenance. We need both if we're to have a chance at having a fulfilled life.

It is a persistent plague of our age that people live at extremes: wealth or poverty, closeness or loneliness, security or trauma. The chasm between those who have more than enough and those who have far too little—often less than they need for basic survival—is disgraceful, but it seems to be always with us. However, this book does not focus on the question of material privilege; instead, we look at the universal human need for emotional closeness and nurturing relationships. But it's essential to point out that our capacity to care about the world around us is directly related to our emotional health. Emotional impoverishment may protect us from the pain of others, but it also diminishes our capacity for love and happiness.

My own, personal record of altruism and care for others has been pretty spotty. There have been times in my life when I was engaged in service and ministry to others in need. But there have also been long periods in which I withdrew from serving. And there is a direct correlation between these periods of serving others and the state of my relationships at the time. When preoccupied with managing *my* worries and struggling with *my* moods, I am self-absorbed and useless to others. In periods of circumstantial calm and emotional equilibrium, I find my capacity to serve others restored.

To those who fear that we have become a culture of the selfish, I would suggest that perhaps our self-absorption more accurately reflects our emotional deprivation. We can work and love best when we are emotionally sustained. The evidence is clear and convincing: There is no substitute for close connection to others for providing the emotional resources that directly benefit each of us. Comfortable or uncomfortable, we are built to thrive by being close to others.

We have each had countless experiences that remind us that being with others offers great comfort. Imagine, for instance, that you're traveling to a strange city. Your flight is delayed, and you land at your destination late at night. You've got directions to your hotel, but once you've left the airport in your rented car, you miss a turn and find yourself hopelessly lost. It starts to rain heavily. You find yourself in a section of town where you don't feel safe. There's no one around to help you or give you directions. You try to turn around and retrace your route, but you can't remember all the turns. You find yourself wondering if you're going to drive all night. What if your car runs out of gas? Even if you could find someone to ask directions from, would you be safe?

Now, imagine the same scenario again, but with one significant difference. You're traveling with a group of close friends. Imagine the change. You'd be talking and laughing. You wouldn't feel afraid to stop and ask for directions, because you wouldn't feel vulnerable and alone. Glenn can attest to this truth because he had this exact same experience. After attending a baseball game at Wrigley Field in Chicago with a few of his friends, he missed a crucial turn on the way home and found himself lost and driving through a rough area of town. In a matter of minutes, his friends were teasing him and laughing. Eventually, they made it back without incident and found the whole experience pretty amusing. Ironically, a few months later, when returning from Chicago alone after attending a convention, Glenn made another navigational mistake. (Glenn really needs a global positioning system when he drives—that, or a navigator.) This time, he was on his own. As he drove through tough neighborhoods, long after midnight, he found his heart starting to pound with anxiety: Would he get home safely? Wandering around Chicago with his friends had been fun. This was being *lost*.

Many, perhaps most, of us could tell similar stories. They reflect a profound truth: When we are surrounded by people we know and with whom we feel connected, their presence mitigates and can even transform the ordinary strains and stresses of life. Even fear feels more like adventure when you are with people you know and love. The harm caused by isolation is often invisible; the symptoms it produces could be ascribed to other, more peripheral causes. We've made some strong assertions in the previous sections. What does the scientific evidence suggest about the matter?

The Emotional Benefits of Being Connected

In comparative studies on levels of job stress and worker dissatisfaction, the data show that the people of individualistic cultures typically report much higher stress levels than do the people of collectivist cultures. In spite of our high standard of living and contrary to what we might suppose, economic privilege is not automatically associated with high levels of life satisfaction and overall emotional well-being. Instead, the sense of *belonging* seems to be closely tied to these desirable states of being. The researchers reporting these studies suggest that this cultural difference is not accidental.

Glenn once supervised a Nigerian student, Gideon, as he finished his master's thesis, so he could return to his home country. Gideon's approach to graduate school was strikingly different from the attitude of his American fellow students. Almost all the social or academic obligations he planned seemed to revolve around the impact his absence was having on his wife and children. Although he was under tremendous pressure to complete his thesis and return to Nigeria, Gideon never emotionally detached from his home and extended family. They were always central to his attention. Before long, Glenn knew all of Gideon's children's names and even spoke with them several times on the phone.

By contrast, even though most of the American students maintained contact with their families, they were far more detached from their home ties and withdrawn into their independent lives. Gideon seemed able to maintain a relaxed and casual spirit—quite a contrast to the stress and tension taken for granted by most American graduate students. The contrast in cultures was apparent and vivid. The close connection to family, the sense of belonging to his relationships, and his culture were far more passionate and sustaining for Gideon. It was also striking how utterly devoted his family seemed to be to his mission. They all were deeply interested in Gideon's endeavors, communicating their support regularly. They were concerned with the ups and downs of his schedule and the setbacks he encountered. By contrast, Glenn has watched numerous American students flame out of graduate school in a whirlwind of stress. Similar observations have been supported in research findings.

In one study of medical students, researchers found that those who were married experienced significantly lower levels of stress than those who were single. Moreover, those single students who got married during the course of the study showed significant decreases in their stress levels when compared to the levels they reported during their single days. The researchers concluded that the results of this study showed evidence for the "protection/support hypothesis." Close family members provide real emotional support. What is it about more closely connected cultures that foster emotional health instead of distress? Gideon's culture values such things as the expression of support and affirmation during hard times. It puts less emphasis on competition and more emphasis on maintaining regular contact with loved ones and feeling tied to a larger group purpose. We could all take a lesson from Gideon about the benefits of sustaining emotional closeness.

The Physical Benefits of Being Connected

Our need for closeness becomes dramatically evident when illness strikes. Like so many other families, the scourge of breast cancer has hit mine. Two women very dear to me have faced this terrifying disease. Of course, we're deeply grateful for sophisticated medical treatments and scientific progress. When cancer is diagnosed, it's obvious that the first step is to get the best medical care available. But research shows that too many patients miss a crucial follow-up in their treatment. Medical care is most effective when joined to a sustained, strong, social and emotional support system.

In the 1980s, a psychiatrist at Stanford University, David Spiegel, conducted research with women diagnosed with breast cancer. Anxiety, depression, and feelings of loss are normal emotional responses to the diagnosis of cancer. Spiegel explored how women diagnosed with breast cancer fared when they talked through these feelings with other women with the same disease. His results are now legendary. After one year, those women who attended weekly peer-group support meetings and talked about their feelings and problems experienced far less anxiety and depression than women who did not attend such groups. Attending a group discussion session just once a week resulted in a much greater ability to cope with the assault of cancer. And emotional strength is associated with physical recovery and health. Spiegel's results shouldn't surprise anyone. When we have a close network of people surrounding us, we feel better. We also cope better.

Bart, a close friend of ours, was stunned by a completely unexpected diagnosis of a life-threatening illness. He had to undergo months of painful treatments at a hospital a thousand miles from his home. His family and friends rallied around to support Bart, his wife, Nancy, and their two daughters. People's names immediately filled up the roster for a day-long blood drive. Several local church congregations actively prayed for him. At the hospital, Bart received hundreds of cards. Their friend Sandy organized an e-mail system to distribute daily updates on Bart's health, provided by Nancy, to some sixty other family members, friends, and co-workers. We were a part of the team. We were doing something together.

Their two young daughters remained home with their grandparents. They went to school and tried to hang on to some small modicum of normalcy while their father endured his therapy. When they were preparing for Christmas and couldn't find their decorations, Sandy sent out an e-mail asking all of us to donate one of our own decorations. In less than forty-eight hours, two overflowing baskets of ornaments were at their front door. All Bart could do was passively receive all this support, prayer, and encouragement.

Bart is recovering and back at work. He told me how overwhelming the support had been for him and his family. He also expressed his fervent belief that his friends' spirited and resolute love and care played a major part in his own determination to fight the disease and get well. He is a changed person, not only because of the trauma of a frightening, debilitating illness, but also because of the animating power of those who surrounded him and showed their love. Having lived in this community for about twenty years, Bart and his family and friendship ties have evolved into a deep network. I've only lived here full-time for about five years. How many people would rally around me? How many people would be there to surround you? Many of us have unwittingly shed our support system and realize it only after we are knee-deep in a major crisis and feel the brunt of our isolation.

Such stories are commonplace in the lives of people everywhere. And they conform to Spiegel's findings about the power of emotional attachment during times of physical crisis. The real kicker in Spiegel's research, however, emerged a full decade later. As it turned out, participation in the weekly discussion groups did a lot more than boost emotions and reduce anxiety. Those women who met weekly and connected with other women in conversation were twice as likely to be alive when Spiegel's research team contacted them for a follow-up study. That's right: *twice as likely to be alive!* Spiegel's results are consistent with the results of many other studies, all of which seem to indicate a very close connection between emotional health and physical health. Emotional depression weakens more than the spirit; it also weakens the immune system.

Try to imagine what would happen if tonight's evening news announced the discovery of a new drug that would double the survival rate of cancer victims over a ten-year period. Such news would undoubtedly be hailed as a major medical breakthrough. Imagine if the very same remedy not only doubled the survival rate of cancer; it also worked in the same way for people with heart disease. The medical data indicate that this might be precisely the case. The 1997 issue of the *Harvard Public Health Review* carried an extended conversation between health experts on the importance of social relationships. Dr. Lisa Berkman, a respected researcher in this area, reported a study of nearly 200 patients who had been hospitalized for myocardial infarction. Over the six-month period following their hospitalization, the people who reported that they had no people they could turn to for social support were *twice as likely* to die as those who reported that they had two or more people they could talk with about their problems. There's that same statistic again showing up in a completely different medical context: *twice as likely.* Berkman concluded that, "Here we have a risk factor related to emotional support that's in the magnitude of the strongest cardiovascular risk factors that we know of."

Spiegel's and Berkman's research has certainly received publicity. We're hearing more and more about the close relationship between emotional and physical health. But this very simple lesson about what we need in order to thrive emotionally and physically still seems to take a backseat to more traditional medical approaches that follow a mechanistic, one-on-one, doctor-to-patient protocol.

In another remarkable study, three psychologists asked nearly three dozen survivors of the Holocaust to spend a few hours with them, recalling their experiences. Most of these survivors shared details that they had never discussed before. Following these sessions, most of the survivors watched themselves on videotape and shared the tapes with family and friends. The researchers discovered that the survivors who had disclosed the most information also made the most significant gains in physical health fourteen months later. In this case, sharing was a healing, health-enhancing experience. This is something we can't do if we don't have someone there to listen.

It isn't something that can always be proven, but it certainly is consistent with the research evidence that the medical community continues to churn out. Social support is strongly related to physical and psychological recovery from illness and disease. And conversely, isolation is related to chronic problems in physical and psychological health.

Stress and Disconnection

Close relationships help us cope better with stress, however it hits us—whether anxiety or depression. It's a truism among health researchers: People with strong social ties also report a greater sense of emotional well-being. One well-known and respected health website, www.broadcasthealth.com, has a reasonable explanation for this phenomenon:

> After all, we evolved as a species in tribal and extended family units in which we lived in close proximity with others. In fact, our survival depended on it: being smaller, weaker, and slower than many

other animals, we learned to rely on our capacity to think, plan, communicate, and band together for mutual protection and support. It is no wonder we naturally seek the support of partners, friends, and family members, not only in times of hardship and stress, but throughout our lives.

The connection between isolation and loss of energy isn't always obvious. But we've all experienced it in our daily lives. Take, for instance, this ordinary scenario: You come home exhausted from a tiring day at work, and all you want is to change into your sweats, flop in front of the tube, and vegetate until you go to bed. But there's a note on the fridge reminding you that you'd said you'd go out to a good friend's engagement dinner that evening. You desperately want to cancel, but you really can't back out. So you force yourself to shower, change, and drag yourself there. Once you arrive, you find yourself starting to perk up; you feel livelier, and you enjoy yourself thoroughly. By the time you get home, several hours later, you notice that you have far more energy than you did when you first got home earlier in the evening. Is this merely a sustained adrenaline rush? Or is your body responding normally to the stimulation of being with others? In reality, both are true.

Engaging in social encounters, especially with friends and close others, unleashes our adrenaline *and* naturally enlivens us. Feelings of drowsiness and fatigue often result from our emotional state, not from any objective drain on our physical stamina. Every therapist has seen a patient becoming drowsy and nodding off in sessions when certain topics are on the table. Anyone who has experienced depression is well aware that sleepiness is not always related to overexertion any more than insomnia results from too much rest.

Many of us notice that when a person suffers a loss, whether it's being fired, having a marriage break up, or losing a loved one, he or she may experience health problems afterward. My wife, Sally, writes and teaches on grief and loss and runs an agency and several support groups. In her experience, there is a powerful, predictable, and obvious correlation between loss, grief, and health problems. Aside from the obvious emotional complications, such as depression and anxiety, many who have suffered loss also develop chronic physical ailments. In situations such as these, have the gods gone crazy, visiting all these afflictions on innocent souls? Or are there more subtle factors at work? The evidence suggests the latter. David Myers, an authority on close relationships, has documented the findings of several major studies on the relationship between health and our connection to other people. One study specifically examined people who had been widowed, divorced, or fired from their jobs. The results clearly showed that after going through these highly stressful events, people were much more susceptible to disease. Just how the immune system is connected to our emotional state is not entirely clear. But the fact of the connection is something that the medical community hardly even debates anymore.

Quantifying the impact of a severe rupture in your close relationships is beyond the realm of science at this point in time. But there are still some provocative clues. Myers tell us of a study in Finland that included 96,000 widowed people. Death among the widowed population was twice as likely in the week following their partner's death than it was for the nonwidowed population. Once again, there's that little statistic popping up: *twice as likely.* And once again, we suggest that an effect of this magnitude is worth shouting about. We need close relationships.

In the film *Lorenzo's Oil,* based on a true story, a young child is diagnosed with a rare brain disorder. All the clinical literature on the disorder pointed to the same verdict: certain death within two years. But Lorenzo didn't die as predicted, and the story of how he survived reminds the viewer repeatedly about the role of family closeness and devotion. While the text of the movie certainly focuses on how persistence can move the medical community toward faster breakthroughs and new developments, it is also about the power of emotional attachment in the healing process.

Families learn this lesson every day when they face crises and illnesses. Even in a disease as serious as leukemia, one study shows that social support from family and friends over a two-year period resulted in a 54 percent survival rate, compared to only 20 percent when the social support just wasn't there. A number of other studies show the same effect also occurs in patients who have suffered heart attacks. Those who have the close connection with others end up healing faster and surviving longer.

The Problem of Intimacy

Why does it seem so difficult for us to really comprehend the message that we do better when we're connected with other people? It's hard for us to imagine that an activity as common and natural as interpersonal discourse is, nonetheless, so central to our emotional health. Physicians find it easier to deal in the familiar domain of pharmacology. In our highly technological age, it may seem too simplistic to suggest that association with others and sharing our feelings is in itself a potent remedy to emotional and even physical distress. But simple as it may be, it seems to be exactly what we need.

Missing this essential point reminds me of an old joke often told in church circles. A minister finds himself stranded in rising floodwaters. A man comes by and throws the pastor a lifeline. But he refuses to grab it, declaring, "I have served God in this community for thirty years. He will save me!" A while later, a rescue boat comes by and the people in it shout to the pastor to get in, but again he refuses, declaring that God will save him. A helicopter then flies over and drops a rope down to the minister; again he refuses and shouts that God will rescue him. And then the waters rise a bit more, and he drowns. Arrived at the gates of heaven, he meets St. Peter and complains bitterly that God didn't save him. St. Peter snaps back, "What are you talking about? We sent you a rope, a boat, and a helicopter!" Too many of us face life with the same stubborn myopia. In our age of increasing isolation and disconnection, we seem to have a hard time recognizing the simple truth that is staring us in the face: *We must acknowledge our dependence and accept that we need each other.*

In the prestigious journal *American Psychologist,* one researcher pointed out that "virtually every study on human happiness reveals that satisfying close relationships constitute the very best thing in life. There is nothing people consider more meaningful and essential to their mental and physical well-being than their close relationships with other people."

If this is indeed the case, shouldn't it be easy for us to tend to our relationships and keep the closeness we need? The answer, sadly, is "no." Cultural forces that we identified earlier make it increasingly difficult to form and maintain close relationships. In addition, we often fail to appreciate the fact that having people around is not the same thing as having close relationships. Merely being surrounded by people does not mean you have real emotional connections with them. What you need are relationships characterized by disclosure, trust, and caring. Casual, superficial contacts don't do the trick and may actually tire us out more than they recharge our batteries, especially if we're introverts who need time and space alone.

The lack of intimacy throws us back onto our immediate families, for lack of any other source of real closeness. Increasingly, we hear that the family unit as a social institution is in crisis. We tend to attribute a host of other social problems to its demise. But perhaps in reality it's the other way around. We may not be suffering from isolation because of the breakdown of the family. Rather, the family may be cracking under the pressure of the increasingly isolated lives of its members. Instead of reducing our own stress levels in order to take the strain off the family, we focus on attachment to family as a way of reducing our stress levels. As Christian writer Henri Nouwen expresses it, "Our loneliness makes us cling to one another, and this mutual clinging makes us suffer immensely because it does not take our loneliness away. But the harder we try, the more desperate we become. Many of these 'interlocking' relationships fall apart because they become suffocating and oppressing."

The Book of Ecclesiastes says, "Two are better than one, because they have a good reward for their toil. For if they fall, one will lift up his fellow; but woe to one who is alone and falls and does not have another to help." As frequently happens, this historical wisdom from the pre-empirical age resonates with modern scientific research findings. Close relationships provide us the crucial moments when we share our pain and allow others to help "bear our burdens."

Just Who Is Our Family?

How would you describe the relationship you have with members of your own family? What words could you use to compare your feeling for a parent, a sibling, or a child to your feeling for a best friend or very close colleague? How would you define the word "intimacy"? Many tend to narrowly associate the word with sexual closeness, but as you can well see, it can be used in a broader sense to mean emotional closeness. Your intimates are the people in your life who are emotionally close, who have refrigerator rights.

Sadly, not all our family relationships are intimate. Sometimes the distance is physical; sometimes it's psychological. For years, I was somewhat estranged from my family in general and my parents in particular. Part of it was harbored resentment over past tensions in our relationship, and part was simply due to physical distance. But although I have come to terms with this and reconciled, it has still taken many years to bridge the emotional chasm that had developed. I still would not characterize my relationship with my parents as emotionally close. But isn't this typical? Millions of people come from families that are not overtly dysfunctional but in which something was amiss. Whether it was a climate of conflict or inhibiting control, they bided their time for their adult freedom. It seemed to me that for everyone I saw in therapy who came from a traumatic childhood, there were three others who were just as estranged from their apparently intact family.

Physical distance makes reconciliation difficult if not impossible. But it can be done. Mark was someone I counseled over a period of years about the problems with his family. He doesn't have warm and sweet memories of his childhood. His unending conflicts with his older, bullying brother combined with his parents' passivity and emotional indifference drove him out of his house to his own independence immediately after college. For years, he found every reason imaginable to minimize contact with his parents and sisters. Having ceased speaking to his brother more than fifteen years earlier, he was on a path of progressive detachment from his parents and sisters. As he tells it:

> When Jean and I relocated a few years back, I unconsciously made sure to be just far enough away to make visiting my family inconvenient. The few visits we had only served to cement this resistance to a relationship. Every slight ever made by my family became an excuse for removing them from my world. I'll bet there are lots of people in this position. In the past I would say I had a relationship with my family, but I would always keep them at arm's length, carefully regulating my contact with them.

Over time, I came to believe that the positives about a close family relationship outweighed the negatives. Gradually, I began to repair the damage done by my detachment and defensive antagonism toward my parents, punishing them for past slights. I found the gumption to speak to them about what I felt and experienced. I was not expecting any immediate change, but it felt great to just make them aware of my feelings. I also began to simply involve myself more in their lives and, in return, to include them in mine. While some of the discomfort remained, something really interesting began to occur. As had been the case earlier in life, the warmth and security of the close family relationships began to return. Over the past few years, I was once again able to share life with them. The strength of these relationships, especially with my sister, has made a huge difference in the quality of my social life and has brought me unexpected peace about my past.

Not everyone has this kind of opportunity. In some instances, after an extended lapse of time our self-absorbed lives can keep old family wounds open and raw for so long that they never close and heal. A friend, Mary, for instance, is close to her mother and younger sister, but her relationship with her father is distant, and her elder brother has had almost nothing to do with his birth family in years. So far from being warm and close, many sibling or parent-child relationships are fraught with strain, disappointment, and pain. I'll bet your own family has stories of lingering estrangement over old unresolved injuries. Every family has an uncle, sister, or parent who checked out and never returned.

We each have experienced sadness when once important relationships have cooled or even died. And we have abandoned hope that, even if we wanted to we could never resurrect our own original family system. We try to compensate for what we miss by trying to fill in the gaps. Because my two brothers live a thousand miles away, for instance, I have needed to create friendships with other men who provide some of what I'm missing from the years of emotional closeness I had with Don and Steve. For many years, I tried to get by relying on casual friendships and passing acquaintances. But these are never adequate. When I recognized the need to replicate some of what I once took for granted from my family, I began to draw myself into closer contact with new friends I had available nearby.

This did not mean merely intensifying an effort to feel more closeness or trying to conjure stronger emotions toward my friends. It did not involve bonding rituals or some other clichéd approach that promises a quick deepening of emotional closeness. After all, that's not how I'd gotten close to my brothers in the first place. If anything, I remember bickering and fighting with them more than I recall "warm-fuzzy" times. I became close to my family members through all our time together: shared hours, days, months, and years of experiences. That sense of shared experience is what gives a thrill to college reunions or regimental get-togethers.

When you find yourself being too much alone and separated from those earlier attachments, you have to start over again. And the same truth applies to new refrigerator rights relationships as to older ones: What they need most is shared experience. It is the commitment of time together that matters, not the commitment to have feelings. The former may be a tedious process that taxes our patience, but the latter approach simply does not work. It takes effort, but many are finding ways to improvise a sense of attachment. As one person told me:

> When I was a kid, we moved about every four years, and the average is about the same now. The loss of relationships is so much a part of my life that I really don't know what to compare it to.

Something that has been important for me and for my children is to have a place that is "home," a special place that doesn't change from year to year and that will still be there after a move. For us, the "home" has become the campsite we go to every year. The same group of families has been going there for about twenty years, and we know the people there better than we ever get to know the people in our neighborhoods. My kids have developed more intense, lasting friendships during their summers than they have at home. My daughter and son-in-law met there and were married right after they graduated. It's funny to think that a summer campsite is where we found a permanent sense of home.

A church can be family. Glenn and I couldn't write about the need for close relationships if we hadn't experienced that need personally and directly. Having spent many years involved in church life, we have seen countless examples of how a close-knit faith community becomes family to its members. Every congregation faces the joys and sorrows of its people. It celebrates weddings and baptisms; it rejoices over graduations and achievements. But it also sustains the ill and injured and their families, and it's there for the dying and for those who mourn. It can be amazing to see a community, knit together not by blood ties but by faith and love, close its ranks around those in need. For all of the public skepticism, for all those who mock and deride "organized religion" or make scathing comments about the sins of the church, in real life, faith communities can make all the difference in the world. Millions of anonymous souls of good heart and strong faith serve and love others in their church, synagogue, or mosque. For them, their "faith family" soothes the loss of close ties to blood kindred.

When my grandson was born critically ill and spent two months in a children's hospital an hour away, our church not only prayed fervently for his healing, they also dropped off dinner at our daughter's house every single night while we were all shuttling back and forth to the hospital. Glenn's own daughter Erin had a terrible scare when she contracted a rare spinal virus that rendered her numb for several weeks. During this time, people from their church showed up virtually every day Erin was in the hospital. The steady stream of visitors communicated a level of support and concern that (Glenn believes) had a definite impact on the emotional health of the family and Erin's physical health as well. Imagine how Glenn and I now feel toward these helpful individuals these many years later. Our bond is strong and continues to deepen its roots through our shared experiences over time.

Making Time

As children, we may have had the luck to grow up in a good family, with stability and secure closeness that we could take happily for granted. What is different in our adulthood is our confounded freedom to dissociate, to be alone, to limit contact to fleeting time and carefully controlled experiences. Now what we need are new commitments, ones that involve sharing time and experience with others and that allow our relationships to grow slowly and solidly. But in today's world, this often feels like an unrealistic and impractical luxury. Where do I find the time and energy to commit for a long-haul relationship outside my marriage, my children, and my work?

I hate to say it, but I have to make that time and energy. There's no fast alternative, and there is no choice—unless, of course your life is really just fine the way it is now. The tension most people report between independence and stability is an ongoing life challenge. It's depicted in the film *It's a Wonderful Life,* in which George Bailey's longing to travel and see the world is constantly frustrated by circumstances beckoning him to remain at home. When sinking into despair, he is shown in a spiritual vision that it is his present life of loving and being loved that is truly the wonderful life. When his wife and children cannot reach him on their own, the love and devotion of his abundant friends rescue George, save his life, and restore his soul. It is the life full of relationships that is the wonderful life. The message is that when you build a complete assortment of relationships, you have everything you need. No wonder millions of us spend a night, sometime around Christmas, getting a little moist around the eyes with both satisfaction and longing as we watch this old film.

But what if we don't have George's encumbrances? Many of us are free to leave—to go off in search of our own wonderful life. The lure to be in a better place is unprecedented in our culture. Television relentlessly brings images of beautiful and exciting lifestyles to us. Like anyone else, I was attracted by the splendor of places like Hawaii or Colorado. But I also longed to live in a house like Beaver Cleaver's, which was a lot nicer than mine. Who among us hasn't grown up eager to act on the freedom to go where our heart beckons? One woman wrote to us and told of the difficulty to follow her heart's desire:

My husband and I have made three vacation trips to San Diego in the past year. We fell in love with the area the first trip and spent the next two trips scouting out the "small towns" surrounding San Diego trying to find just the right spot. Our third trip we attended our San Diego friend's wedding and met many locals who were friendly and actually invited us to dinner while we were in town. I have no problem making friends, and although we will be leaving our friends here, I am positive we will make new friends in California.

Some of our Illinois friends and mostly our family have chastised us for our future plans to relocate. Protests range from . . . "It's so expensive out there," "Aren't you afraid of earthquakes, you can't get insurance, you know," "How can you leave your job and start over?" My husband's out-of-state sisters advised us to "wait until Mom is gone before you leave her here alone in Illinois." My mother, who is so emotionally dependent on me, just cries every time I try to put "replacement me" people into place to help her. Both of my siblings live out of state also and have not spoken to our mother for more than a year. We continue to put our ducks in a row to complete this move, but emotionally we are both being drained.

Pop culture tells us that a wonderful life includes a rewarding career, financial success, the right home, the right possessions, a good marriage, and successful, happy kids. Our staggering patterns of geographic mobility are not indicative of aimless meandering. Rather, they are associated with a quest for self-improvement, positive change, all directed at attainment, achievement, and fulfillment. But maybe what we need most is what George has and many of us lack. Close emotional ties may chafe sometimes, but they also bind. We need connection. We need to feel at home again. We need to know that the support will be there whenever we need it.

We need refrigerator rights.

Points to Remember

❖ Human beings are wired for connection. Scientific research clearly shows the emotional and physical health benefits of being tightly connected to other people. Social support from relationships has been linked to surviving cancer, beating depression, and surviving heart problems.

✧ One of the first steps in conquering our social isolation is to readily acknowledge what the research community has known for years: We literally need each other to survive.

✧ While we may become separated from our family of origin, we still need fathers, mothers, brothers, sisters, aunts, uncles, nephews, and nieces. We need to rebuild our lost families by forging connections with other people who can step into those roles.

We Need to Resist
the Self-Help Fantasy

*By declaring that man is responsible and must actualize the
potential meaning of his life, I wish to stress that the true
meaning of life is to be discovered in the world rather than
within man or his own psyche, as though it were a closed
system.*

—VICTOR E. FRANKL, *Man's Search for Meaning*

You may readily acknowledge the need to have emotional closeness
with others. But you also know from harsh experience that these
very relationships are frequently the source of life's most painful suf-
ferings. Maybe you are there now in the midst of a chaotic marriage, at odds with a child or parent, or locking horns with a boss
or co-worker. The truth is that in our age of deep disconnection,
the few relationships we do have are often rubbed raw by overex-
posure and excessive dependency. We rely on too few people. As a
result, the relationships we do have are often complex. In the struggle to become better equipped as a spouse, employee, friend, or
supervisor, we American achievers seem to be constantly working
on improving our selves.

Into this void pours an ocean of resources about how to remake
every facet of your inner and outer life. We refer to this material
collectively as "self-help." Much of it seems plausible enough, based

on the latest psychological and medical information. For example, Steven Covey's book, *The 7 Habits of Highly Effective People,* is a landmark best-seller. In it, he takes a unique approach to lifestyle and productivity motivation. Covey suggests that if we wander through life without a clear vision or set of goals, we cannot properly organize or effectively structure our time. If we have not defined our purpose and goals, we cannot hope to achieve anything other than what comes our way by accident. But the work of defining our purpose, Covey contends, demands that we work primarily on our personal character. Without the willpower that comes with high character, we will be like rudderless boats in the ocean.

Based on the assumption that many of us feel overwhelmed by commotion and disorder in daily life, Covey suggests that we stop the madness and begin anew. He has gone so far as to incorporate his philosophy about effective living into the popular personal organizing and planning system known as the *Franklin Planner.* By following the proscribed system of listing and prioritizing daily tasks in accordance with your larger goals and vaunted purposes, you are promised a more productive and ultimately more fulfilled life. Best of all, you will feel the effects immediately. This approach to daily living is not some pie-eyed promise, but is based on an extensive review of the literature on effective living. Rooted in time-tested human experience, the approach converts your loftiest ambitions into concrete, workable routines. Covey is right that identifying with these characteristics and putting them into practice will insure you a life of rich psychological and spiritual quality. In short, his system works.

His system works, of course, presuming you continue to use it, and in particular, that you have the dogged discipline to sustain his approach. Many have discovered that the real trick is applying the method every day, without fail, for the rest of your life. I am the perfect candidate for the Franklin-Covey system. My life is hectic, and my skills at organization are weak. I have used my planner in accordance with the prescribed method, and it has helped a lot. But to be honest, if you reviewed my planner over the past year, you'd find that I apply the method less than half the time. For every calendar page showing my tasks neatly laid out, there are at least a couple blank pages following. I know I'm being lax and am failing. Sometimes I think I hear Steven Covey's voice saying, "You can do better than this!" If he saw how poorly I use his wonderful system, he'd probably want to slap me. I feel badly about it, naturally, but I just can't seem to stay the course. If I were grading myself, I would do no better than a "C" in planning. This is hardly good enough to move up the food chain, let alone the ladder of personal fulfillment.

But I know I'm not alone. Many other well-intentioned strivers have a hard time sticking with a self-help book's recommended system. We may have passionately embraced the ideas but have a difficult time keeping it in practice over the long haul. Although nobody's conducted any surveys that we know of, Glenn and I are willing to bet that for every person who faithfully adheres to a self-management program, there are at least three others who continually fall off the wagon. However, if the flaw isn't with these books or programs, what's the inescapable conclusion? The problem must be with *me*. I must be incompetent and incapable of adhering to even the most obvious plan for better living.

Every day, in thousands of meetings held by businesses and organizations, workers are cajoled and excited to produce ever-greater results for their company. Companies bring in motivational speakers to tell employees how they can increase their productivity. The common theme is "You have *within yourself* everything necessary to create and sell even more than you have in the past." The focus of attention is usually on individual effort. Even when the rhetoric includes terms such as "team" and even "family," the locus of change remains on the individual worker: "If it's going to be, it's up to me," as the motivational button puts it. The prevailing philosophy is individual contribution to the team. "The team is not here to help you; you are here to help the team." If you don't perform, not only are you not up to snuff, but you're letting the team down. Talk about guilt! On more than one occasion I've seen how this approach only increases workers' anxiety levels. For instance, one time when I was speaking at an annual meeting of top sales performers for a large company, the CEO said that the company had its best year ever. But he then cautioned me that many in the audience were feeling great pressure to repeat the performance. "It's getting harder to win, and they're worried." So they bring in motivators who refer to the enormous untapped potential of the human being. Believing that each of us is like a grand and mighty engine, we are encouraged to believe in our underused power. *I have fantastic, albeit dormant aptitude to do so much more than I believe I can accomplish.*

Using this power-plant metaphor, an unfulfilled life is an untested life, a failure to *step on the gas,* so to speak. By only idling our engines, we live below our capacity; we fail to fulfill our potential and reap the rewards we deserve. In this view, stress is, perhaps, a self-inflicted condition and the consequence of a limited vision and diminished expectations. Much like my drill sergeant, the motivator rejects "whining" and makes no concessions to discouragement. Although I may feel tired and overwrought, this is just an illusion. In fact, I am simply choosing to live below my potential, operating at a small percentage of my capacity. Like an idle nuclear power plant, my seemingly small self can ignite a vast eruption of productivity. My body's computer actually *is* in sleep mode.

Or at least, that's the story. But is it a true story?

Resisting the Culture of Self

Based on what we have outlined in this book thus far, it should be clear that we believe the problem of personal change is rooted in lost relationships, not lack of motivation, energy, or personal will. It is in the absence of refrigerator rights relationships that we turn to fast, available resources. To replace the missing voices of mothers and fathers and other trusted family members, we turn to ourselves with a little help from the popular culture.

The marketplace of ideas abounds with resources designed to help us feel better and live the good life. You can find resources to help you improve yourself in every possible way, whether you want to be richer, more sexually fulfilled, more physically fit, a better salesperson or manager—even a more effective church pastor. This isn't a bad thing. We really do need to know ourselves and to find out where and how we need to change. It makes good sense that to accomplish my goal of becoming the best person I can be; I should work on myself. That, we are told, is the true path to peace and happiness. But in this ocean of material, we are hard-pressed to find much about the loss of refrigerator rights relationships. The focus of self-help and popular psychology is me. And why not? "Me" is where I live.

When I wake up each morning, the day is mine to negotiate personally, or so I believe. I lie in bed and think about what I have planned and who I may see. My day is anchored in my own personal experience. I experience life from the inside out, from the point of view of my own solitary self. Evolving myself supercedes other goals, even if the goal is to form better relationships. We have come to accept the idea that we change from the inside out. If I am isolated, I have no option but to take on the task of personal change from within myself. No matter how many self-help books and tapes I consume, an empty social environment will not yield the kind of personal growth I desire. We don't stop to examine our presupposition that personal change is supposed to come first and relationships are at best secondary. It's as if to say, *I'm essentially alone, so it is completely up to me to construct my fulfilled life.*

But good and worthy as this goal is, it misses something fundamental. Although we fervently desire to change from the inside out, personal change is actually initiated from the outside in—by our environment and the input we get from others. And no matter how cogent and perceptive a self-help strategy is, it is always speaking to me individually. Contrast the wisdom of a book by an author who doesn't know you from Adam with the counsel of your mother, sister, or uncle. No comparison. Unless, of course, you don't have access to such emotionally close relationships. If that's the case, you are left with what you can buy. And it's always a poorer substitute. We need *personalized* good advice to help us see ourselves truthfully. It's fine for the experts to promise better, more intimate relationships if we improve ourselves, but how is that going to happen if we have no relationships to improve?

Relationships with others are often not so much an integral part of me as much as they are an attachment, an extension of my self. I live as a sole individual amidst other individuals. And so my expectation is that the predominant responsibility for my personal happiness rests with me. As I stated in the previous chapter, I live with the illusory expectations that *I must be in control; I am master of my universe.*

Fixing My Past, Fixing My Present

Popular culture has made the term *dysfunctional family* famous. Although the exact criteria are fuzzy, the term *dysfunctional family* usually applies to families that are plagued by a chronic inability to provide stability and security to those in the household. Worse, the dysfunctional family seems incapable of providing its children with a safe, nurturing environment that develops their whole character and teaches them right from wrong. Chaotic and incompetent families have become a staple for talk shows, soap operas, and films. Maybe you come from a family with problems. Given the grim record of marital instability in our society, chances are you might have been raised in a home by a single parent, a stepparent, or perhaps a grandparent. Peculiar though your situation may have been, perhaps it was a nurturing environment nonetheless. There are countless patchwork and nontraditional families that are full of love and under the supervision of able adults. And of course, we have all encountered families who appear perfect on the outside and yet are privately living in a hell of addiction or abuse. Whatever form your early family took, you can look back and recognize that your childhood story was either pleasant or pain-filled. Whichever it was, you have come through it and here you are.

It seems perfectly plausible to assume that our childhood environment is a lead factor in shaping who we have become. Certainly, it is an axiom in psychotherapy that our childhood experiences are intimately connected to our present level of emotional well-being. If you're one of those who has come from a complicated family and survived to tell the tale, understanding your own history helps you to make more sense of the problems in your life. You can see how you arrived at the emotional state you are in now and that gives you some clues about what problems you have to tackle.

The search to understand my feelings of discontent customarily takes me down one of two paths. One goes back into my past and is based on a perception that my present woes are rooted in hurtful early experiences, perhaps even traumatic events. The second takes me into my interior as I feel it now and attributes current ill feelings to present circumstances and stressors. At different times I travel down each one in turn, seeking clarity and discernment, and each path reveals something to me, about me. Self-search helps make sense of my identity. Learning to understand what shaped me in the past and what is pressing on me now helps me form and cultivate my character.

When determined to improve my lot in life, particularly my own mental or emotional state, I begin by trying to ascertain what factors have brought me to my current situation in life. How did I get where I am? Tying my present dysfunction to my early family dysfunction is a logical tendency. It is tempting to ascribe *any* current life problem I'm having to some lingering effect from my horrible past. Mental health professionals correctly sense the strong connection between chaotic family life and many adult psychiatric problems. Patterns of addiction, personality disorders, abuse, and criminal, antisocial pathology are often suspected as an outgrowth of being raised in a virulent family environment.

But as sensible as it may seem for a person from a bad family to focus on the past to explain present problems, this focus may be overstated and even misguided. For example, we often hear about the consequences of being raised in an alcoholic family. The studies warn that if you come from a family with an alcoholic parent, you are at increased risk of becoming an alcoholic yourself. Studies show that if your father was *not* an alcoholic, you are at a 5 percent risk of becoming alcohol dependent yourself. By comparison, if your father *was* an alcoholic, the odds soar to 20 percent. Children of alcoholics are also more likely to marry into families in which alcoholism is prevalent. Yikes! To hear this is certainly frightening for any child of an alcoholic. The same risk holds for those who come from families with a pattern of domestic violence or sexual abuse. Hearing these reports, it's easy to fear that your personal history puts you at risk—that regardless of your own attempts, you are doomed to reenact your family's pathology.

But if we take a closer look at the numbers in these studies, the picture is less frightening. Depending on which studies you consult, anywhere from 13 to 25 percent of children of alcoholics become alcoholics themselves. That leaves 75 to 87 percent who do *not* become alcoholics. Clearly *most* children from families with alcoholic members will fall into this group. Although it is prudent for children of alcoholics to beware, it is unnecessary to despair. You are not fated or doomed. But because of your known personal history, coupled with public rhetoric and hype, you may overidentify with your family's own particular dysfunction.

To what degree do the nonaddicted, grown children of addicts still conclude that all the problems they confront in life are grounded in their parent's disease? While this position is certainly understandable, in most cases it is wrong. It's as unhelpful to overestimate the impact of the past as it is to ignore it. Pop culture is filled with voices telling me to search my past to discover what's ailing me. But by overfocusing on the casualties of poor parenting, we risk missing all those people who survived disruptive families and later blossomed into cheerful adults and excellent parents. The happy truth is that millions of people overcome a stormy childhood. There is growing evidence to suggest that we are more resilient than we might have previously believed. In their landmark book on the effects of divorce, *For Better or For Worse,* E. Mavis Hetherington and John Kelly argue that not all children suffer negative effects when their parents divorce. It isn't that simple. While adolescents appear to be at a higher level of risk, some children actually seem to thrive after their parents split.

Glenn developed a bleeding ulcer in high school that hospitalized him for two weeks and put him on a diet of milk and Maalox. At the time of the attack, ulcers were thought to originate from stress and anxiety. Today, doctors know that a major cause is a bacterial infection that can be treated routinely with antibiotics. Contrary to his instincts, Glenn lived for years with the belief that, despite whatever he consciously thought, he was keeping his emotions repressed and letting them eat away at his stomach. But although he eventually learned about the medical breakthrough, his parents have never quite gotten the message. For years, whenever Glenn communicates with his parents and seems calm and placid, they warn him about aggravating his ulcer—a condition that he has been free from for the past thirty years! Glenn's parents got into the habit of seeing his entire personality through the lens of past problems. It has proven to be a tough habit to break. Many of us tend to do the same thing.

In a society that so forcefully emphasizes self-help and individual overcoming, I'm always being prodded to solve my life problems by fixing what must be wrong with me. But maybe, just maybe, that's not the real problem.

What's Wrong with Me?

If you are from an intact, good enough family and yet still feel strong emotional stress and strain, to what do you ascribe your condition? Therapists refer to people like you as the "worried well." A high percentage of clients seeking relief in psychotherapy are such as these. There are many who, amidst prosperity and good fortune, are unhappy. Often, the problems center around their complicated relationships with their significant others, whether a spouse, a parent, or a child. The stress felt in the lives of individuals and families who might appear "functional" and even successful drives them in every direction seeking help and relief. This is certainly my story.

I come from an allegedly functional family. My parents have been married more than fifty-five years. Although they both went back to college and my mother went on to earn two master's degrees, during my childhood, she was a domestic engineer and a full-time presence. Her lifestyle might have looked life June Cleaver's, but I was no Wally. Picture what would have happened to June's personality if she had Eddie Haskell for a son. There you go. She was tough and vigilant and a ceaseless disciplinarian. Always on duty, she seemed to always be awake. She was active before I woke up and after I went to sleep. As a working-class family, we did not have much money. But like many from a less-than-privileged background, I was blissfully unaware of any cash flow problems gnawing at my parents each month. We had presents under the Christmas tree, a touring or camping vacation each summer, and an instilled compassion for the less fortunate. And I always assumed that there were millions of these. I knew we weren't rich, but I knew we weren't poor. We had our challenges, but we were functional. As a result, I have never seriously considered that any of my stress or psychological discomfort was connected to my past. Although it wasn't perfect, it was certainly good enough.

People who, like me, were raised in a reasonably loving and emotionally sturdy family tend to link current problems not to the past but to present pressures and circumstances. It might be problems with the boss or office politics. Sometimes it's rebellious kids, conflict with our spouse, or health and financial worries. When I'm faced with these problems, my first instinct is to triage the problem by resolving it or simply by making it *go away*. To do this, I usually turn into a "management expert"; in other words, I resort to being a "control freak." I think, "I'm smart, I'm bright, I'm capable, I can manage this."

I keep forgetting, of course, that maybe what I need to manage isn't the problem itself, but my own irritable reaction to it. And it often doesn't occur to me that I'm irritable because I'm usually facing my problem on my own, without much support. Sure, I have Sally, but I'm conscious of not burdening her with all my worries. She has her own problems to face. Where else can I turn? It's amazing how it just doesn't readily occur to me that I need an available support system for my life to work, especially when times are tough.

Janet told us about the crisis she faced with her cancer:

> When I came home from the doctor after being handed my diagnosis of breast cancer, I had several checklists of things to do. Looking back, I now know that what I needed most was the presence of a strong community of loving support to help me keep going. The practical steps were important and helpful. And they gave me something to focus my mind on when I wandered into scary areas of thought. I concentrated on carefully managing my diet, exercise, and check-up routine. But the real emotional challenge—the fear—which was the worst part early on, was beyond my ability to handle by myself. No matter how many books I read, I couldn't shake the fear. It was my mother, my sister, and the women at my church who helped me cope with my feelings. Thank God for them!

All too often, even if I have a sense of the importance of connecting with others, it may seem too difficult to pursue that goal while I'm still wrestling a whole swamp full of alligators. So I lurch from crisis to crisis, increasingly exhausted and shorter-fused, because I'm trying to fix everything all by myself. It is at this pivotal point that people from functional and dysfunctional families find themselves in the same fix. As different as our personal histories might be, we are all living in an isolating, atomized culture that reinforces physical separation without regard for the emotional consequences. What joins us all is the rigor of the modern lifestyle and the distance we have from family intimacy. More than the particulars of our past or present, it is our disconnection that diminishes our ability to sustain meaning in daily living. The personal isolation that we feel, either from our dysfunctional past or from present circumstances, has the same impact on all our lives.

More than anyone else, mental health professionals know that mood and personality disorders are rampant in our society. In spite of our comfort and privilege, we don't seem to know how to feel better and act more lovingly. Every day, pharmacies dole out truckloads of medication to calm down the hyper and uplift the despondent. Even those of us who don't have to struggle with a clinically diagnosable disorder often complain of vague, uncomfortable feelings: agitation, frustration, unhappiness, and discontent. But the symptoms seem too mild to drive us to get treatment or help. Our stress detracts from our productivity and the quality of our life. It contributes to marital discord and divorce, strains our relationships with our children, and holds us back in our work life.

How should I respond to my discomfort? Like anyone else, I want to get myself back on track, to fix myself when I start to break down. And as I mentioned earlier, there are thousands of books and tapes available to help me improve myself. These sources can help me diagnose my psychological problems and help guide me through a self-directed program of change. No fuss, no muss. A lot of this stuff promises a quick fix. A lot of it is organized in a step-by-step manner to make the path to health and happiness easy to follow. It's fulfillment for dummies.

But the question remains, has it changed you in lasting ways? Maybe it works if you're talking about the mechanics of changing your golf swing or installing a backyard patio. But if you are hoping for psychological growth or even lasting habit formation, this stuff is a dead end. You cannot change yourself by reading a book or watching a tape. Even if you are riveted and inspired by what you read or hear, you won't become different on your own without the ongoing input and support of other people close at hand.

Getting Help

Another alternative, of course, is to get professional help. If you go for counseling or therapy, you do indeed increase the odds of changing yourself in ways that you desire. What many people do not realize, however, is that the process of therapy is rooted in the relationship between the two people—therapist and patient. The therapist can certainly offer wisdom and practical advice at certain moments, but what helps you change in psychotherapy is the relationship itself, not the intellectual acuity of the therapist. Hard as it is to believe, you can be smarter than your therapist and still have the process work. In this way it is reminiscent of your relationship with your grandfather, aunt, or kindly neighbor. They may be dumber than you, but their life experience, larger perspective, and loving posture toward you enables you to grow and develop under their mentoring.

Most mental health disciplines share a similar perspective. It is an orientation toward human problems referred to as the "biopsychosocial" approach. The term may be a mouthful but is an elegant description that reminds the therapist that most of the problems that plague a person have biological, psychological, and social components. Depression is a good example. It is an illness with a *biological* basis that results in a powerful *psychological* effect and debilitating *social* consequences. It is, thus, best treated in all its facets. To only treat one ignores important realities. This is why the treatment of choice for a depression is medication (biological) along with talk therapy (psychological) aimed to reintegrate the person back into their relational life (social).

My own restlessness always seemed weird to me, but it was a symptom whose origins was solved in psychotherapy. It is a little bit of my biology: I have a quick-running metabolism that sits there like a car running in the driveway. It is a little bit of my psychology:

I put up defensive barriers to cope with my fear of losing myself in an intimate attachment. And it's a little bit of my sociology: I grew up with a large, intense family in a small house, and keeping some distance and personal space became a critical social value for me.

It's no surprise that I have always longed to be a more placid person. In my mind and heart I do wish to become more calm and serene. But the truth is, I have to work very hard to confine my impatience and anger. I've compromised by trying to direct it constructively through work and recreation—like steering into a skid instead of just slamming on the brakes. But while my higher thoughts seek after peace and love, my viscera often move me toward the martial arts. I do most deeply admire St. Francis of Assisi, but unfortunately, I have the impulses of *Dirty Harry.* I aspire to be like Master Caine of *Kung Fu:* "I am enlightened and deeply at peace, but if I need to, I can kick you into a bloody pulp in thirty seconds or less without changing my facial expression or raising my heart rate." I don't know what the feminine equivalent is for this dualism, but I'm sure there is one.

Therapy helped me disentangle many of my mysterious habits, impulses, and feelings. But with all its penetrating deconstruction and awesome revelations, five years of therapy did not significantly alter the habits that often impede me in my relationships and work. Therapy made the habits clear, but they did not fully dissipate. What a discouragement. And for years I assumed that the fault was mine: *I must be a bad patient who didn't do my therapy correctly.* Although this is certainly true in some respects, the problem wasn't entirely my doing. Some of it rests with the false expectations about what therapy is and can accomplish.

As much as psychotherapy helped open my eyes to my past and present, it did not bring me to a place where I feel a lot better most days. Yes, I know better *why* I feel the way I do. But I can't change *how* I feel. And my dogged determination to apply Dr. Covey's wisdom through the use of my *Franklin Planner* can give me a measure of where I fall short in planning and organization. But by itself, individually applied, it will not make me a more structured individual. Psychotherapy, popular psychology, and the vast sea of self-help resources available to me are wonderful tools, but they can never work as a singular act of my own effort.

I cannot fix myself. I don't think you can either. We are fixed only and most certainly when we experience daily life surrounded by a diverse array of refrigerator rights relationships.

Points to Remember

- If we're isolated, it seems only natural to attempt to solve our problems alone. But the solution to the problem of isolation can't be found within ourselves. It must come from being with others.

- We often turn to "self-help" when we realize we have a problem. But in the case of our social isolation, it isn't "self-help" that we need. It's help from others. The solution to our problem is not to be found within ourselves. Instead, it is to be found outside ourselves.

- In fact, most "self-help" attempts probably don't work that well. For every person who faithfully adheres to a self-management program, we think there are at least as many others who continually fall off the wagon. The most successful strategies for changing harmful behaviors like alcohol addiction and obesity are to be found in twelve-step programs that situate the individual in a group. The most effective way to change yourself is to reach out to others.

Now What?

"Losing family obliges us to find new family."

—*Finding Forrester*

What a Mess!

By now, it should be clear how strongly I feel about the loss of refrigerator rights relationships. The loss has come about gradually and subtly over the last few decades through a colluding series of social changes. And by now you know, too, how this loss has dramatically altered our culture and diminished our emotional health. I can summarize these changes in three points:

1. We have moved away from our family and places of origin and are increasingly cut off from the important early relationships that helped form our adult character.

2. We have followed our culture's natural course toward self-reliant individualism and personal independence—values that have led us down the trail of busyness, overcommitment, career, and material striving.

3. We have filled in the time we normally would devote to relationships with a number of distractions, especially the electronic media.

As a result, we are socially isolated. We have only ourselves to rely on in managing our daily worries and fears. And because we are not made to cope with emotional isolation, we are getting sicker, both individually and as a society. Our levels of depression, anxiety, and antisocial conflict are already shocking, and they are increasing at an alarming rate. All this trouble feeds on itself, because the strangers from whom we are feeling so alienated in our daily encounters are the very people we desperately need to alleviate our alienation.

What little personal contact we do have with others is fleeting, fast-paced, and shallow: the "soccer mom" friends commiserating while sitting in the stands cheering on the team or the regular weekly golf partner chatting between swings. There is rarely time for talking afterward because you need to get to work or the next activity. So we tolerate friendships that are flimsy and superficial, and we believe that because we have so many of them, we must be socially connected. Instead of getting closer, we find it easier to distract ourselves. Soothing and numbing "screens" lure us and trick us into believing that we are connected to the world. But, in fact, they only serve to postpone the difficult and protracted process of connecting with other real people.

If this profile describes your life, the question is "What do I do now?" If I have lost my refrigerator rights relationships, how do I recover them? My choices are clear and obvious. I can either move back home, to the place and the people of my origins, or I can get about the work of reestablishing new family where I am now. The first choice—moving back—has, in fact, been an option for some, and we spoke with many who have managed to do just that. But I would guess that for most of us, there is no real "home" left. No one I know still lives in the town where I grew up. Too many people have moved; change has been too much a constant for too long. My hometown is mostly just a memory, not a reality I can recover.

Many, perhaps most, of us face the prospect of rebuilding refrigerator rights from the ground up. But what does this entail? It means building a family—a full set of the roles and relationships we imagine in a complete family. This is not some idealistic fantasy. It is an achievable reality. No family is perfect; none is ideal. Some families are more cohesive than others and better able to sustain a stable and secure environment for its members. Regardless of whether you flourished in an ideal family or escaped a horrible one, your task remains the same in adulthood: You need to pull together a whole family of real people. They don't have to be perfect—just a reasonable fit for you. They don't need to be ideal personalities— just ordinarily caring, committed people, warts and all.

A family means more than simply a collection of temperamentally compatible peers. In the ideal, it includes a loving father and mother, brothers and sisters, aunts and uncles, children, grandmother and grandfather, and nieces and nephews. It's a complement of relationships that relate to me in a wide variety of ways. With some I am needy and dependent. With others I am a mentor and source of wisdom, strength, and protection. For some I serve as the source of emotional and physical security. Others serve as my protectors. In all, I am surrounded, ensconced, and known. I belong. The goal of rebuilding a refrigerator rights family is to establish all of those relationships. Can it be done? I think so. I think all these people are all around us if we just look and make the effort.

If we want examples of rebuilding, they're there in the popular culture. The quote at the beginning of this chapter came from the movie *Finding Forrester*, in which the character William Forrester is an agoraphobic recluse who was once a brilliant and famous writer. His isolation led him to a writer's block that lasted thirty years. His unexpected rescue comes through a gifted teenager who crashes into his life from the mean streets below his Bronx apartment. The slow incubation of a father-son relationship brings William out of his painful isolation and saves him at his life's end.

Another of my favorite examples is the film *Steel Magnolias* and its depiction of life in a small southern town and the bond created among a half-dozen women. No two of these women are alike or even compatible. But over the course of many years of life, crossing paths around town and at the beauty salon they all patronize, they become closer than they realize. It isn't until one of the women dies of an asthma attack that they became aware of the emotional bond that's arisen among them.

Two points of *Steel Magnolias* really stood out for me. First, the movie reminds us that our culture puts far too much emphasis on temperamental compatibility and lifestyle conformity as criteria for emotional closeness with others. As we become more both segmented and more homogenous as a society, we fail to appreciate the blessed diversity of life—the rich array of different personalities and personal styles that surround us. It's one thing to make every McDonald's restaurant meet the same set of standards. It's another to push people in that same direction. Diversity means more than racial or ethnic tolerance. We need to resist the temptation to expect all our friends to be just like us. Every family has its eccentrics, and each person we love has traits that drive us crazy sometimes. If we want to rebuild our lost families we have to be ready to embrace—and, dare I suggest, enjoy—all sorts of types, temperaments, and styles.

The second point illustrated in the film is the reminder that becoming emotionally close to others is a process that occurs over time and through shared experience. It is not instantaneous! One myth of our current pop-psychology culture holds that emotional closeness comes about from our focused effort, that it happens in face-to-face encounters. When we look into each other's eyes, we begin to form a bond. But this was not how you became close to members of your own family. In real life, closeness happens as you stand together, as you walk through life shoulder-to-shoulder, keeping each other company. Often, we don't even pay any attention to our real attachments to the people we love. Only at certain moments of sadness or celebration, conflict or passion, do we really understand the depth and importance of our bond. Before the young woman's death, the women in *Steel Magnolias* were primarily aware of the peculiarities and eccentricities of each other—of the differences that separated them. Trauma suspended this awareness and caused them to turn face-to-face, standing together in love and support of each other—like a family.

When I was a young teenager, my sister Joan married Matt, who left for a year in Vietnam shortly after the wedding. Joan stayed with us and gave birth to their first son, Matthew, while still living with our family. You can imagine what a dramatic year this was for her. But even as I went about the dull routine of school life, my sister's experience was a big part of my own life drama. I had no active role to play, but it was a headline event for all of us in the family. I walked alongside my sister with little apparent purpose—just the annoying kid brother, another member of the family. But now, years later, this experience is something I share with my sister—although we never mention it to each other. Even through separation and sometimes conflict, it's in the background, and the bond of closeness I feel with Joan and Matt and her family still holds. It cannot be undone.

Building New Family

If you are socially and emotionally isolated, creating a family is Job Number 1 for you. While it may seem like a daunting task, there are plenty of clues about how you go about it. The important thing to remember is that you don't build family solely through intentions and commitment. The process needs time, and it needs lots of ordinary life experiences, some of them dramatic, but most mundane.

Think of the people you see at least once a week. They might be co-workers, members of your church or club, people you see at the PTA, or neighbors you sometimes chat with. If you gathered them all together, can you picture getting to know them better? Can you imagine them getting to know *you* better? Maybe you already have the beginnings of a family at your fingertips. Maybe you don't.

Would it help if you thought a bit about what constitutes a family? What makes a gathering or collection of people feel like family? Try this on as a possibility: A family is a social environment that:

1. Nurtures commitment and belonging

2. Tolerates and manages conflict

3. Facilitates personal growth and change

Do these criteria describe (at least potentially) the relationships you have with the friends and acquaintances living near and interacting with you regularly? Or do they only fit the past—a family from which you are now separated and see sporadically or not at all? Since you left home, have you chosen to attach in ways that feel close enough to share refrigerator rights as defined by these characteristics? Or have you put your energy elsewhere?

Before we consider each of these ideas in their turn, we have to confront an obstacle: our cherished freedom. We are perfectly free to remain as we are—separated, fiercely individualistic, and isolated. We can give in to our impulses and chase after what we think we most desire, and in the process, we can squander our freedom on shortsighted choices. Our very freedom allows us to choose daily: the Internet or a phone call, the television or dinner with friends, being alone or having a barbecue. But emotional closeness demands more than this. Modern Americans tend to shun entanglements, avoid or plow into conflict, and view growth and change as a private, personal enterprise. Moreover, the notion of seeking out new close relationships is often viewed as complicated, constricting, and threatening. We have been encouraged by our lifestyles and popular culture to move away from entanglements—away from refrigerator rights relationships. But the answer is to push ahead with engagement—to belong in spite of conflict. Only then can we grow.

Nurturing Commitment and Belonging

When I was a graduate student, training to become a therapist, Professor Carol Meyer, an eminent scholar at the Columbia University School of Social Work, told our class about the research that had been done on the family. She said that after many years of studies on what constitutes a "family," the conclusion boiled down to "a simple, clear feeling that you belong." A feeling of belonging is the foundation for experiencing refrigerator rights. With your family of origin, that feeling is inherent even if you can't stand to be around your kin. With new friendships, the growing closeness reaches a particular point at which you and the other person cross a line, and you find yourself with a sense of belonging with that person. For instance, the relationship I have with my stepchildren, Tamara and Tom, grew over time, so that I now have a sense that I belong to them and they to me.

Belonging is a feeling, and we usually know when it's real. We intuitively know the difference between belonging to a family and simply being cordially welcomed among them. You've probably been invited a few times to someone else's family gathering. I've been to a few weddings and family reunions where everyone was having a great time. But they were having a better time than I was. It's not that I wasn't warmly welcomed; everyone was friendly and hospitable. But there was a clear feeling that I wasn't on the inside. I didn't know the jokes, the stories, or the shared history. I didn't understand the meaningful facial expressions or the silent cues. I wasn't really part of the group. Being warmly received is not the same thing as belonging.

Being raised in a house that was so crowded and hectic, naturally I couldn't wait to grow up and get away. I craved more space with less yelling and was forever chomping at the bit, waiting to grab some personal freedom. And for a full decade into my adulthood, I was happy to keep my distance from my parents. Yet in all that time, I never once questioned whether I belonged to my family. I always knew I did, even though my contact with them was only intermittent for many years. So it is with most of us I suspect. Over the few years, when I was practicing as a therapist, many of the people who came to me were wrestling with complex family problems. Often, it was such a constant source of pain that they desperately wanted to get away. But here, too, I noticed that my clients always felt that they were part of their families—that they belonged.

Moving away from your home and family disrupts your sense of belonging. It doesn't matter how gregarious and amicable you are with the new people you meet. You don't begin new relationships with a sense of belonging. In fact, when you are new in town, you seldom belong with anyone outside those who accompanied you on the move. No wonder we cling so desperately to our spouses and children—they are usually all we have.

Like you, I have certainly had anecdotal experiences of belonging. When I was a comedian in New York I belonged to the community of comedians. We worked at night in the comedy clubs and slept most of the day, kind of like bats. Our lifestyle was so out of the ordinary that we developed a strong bond among ourselves. Even on nights when we each performed at different comedy clubs around the New York area, it became our tradition to return to the Comic Strip Comedy Club and hang out late into the night. Sometimes, well after midnight, we would walk over to First Avenue and have breakfast at a twenty-four-hour diner. We became close, and although our careers and choices have separated us all, we remain attached to this day.

Perhaps you have had this experience with bonds you developed in your childhood neighborhood or in college or perhaps the army. You know that feeling of always belonging, no matter how long it's been since you were together. This is the belonging that makes you a family. This is what many of us are missing and longing for in our lives today. If you set out to recover your refrigerator rights relationships, your goal is to evolve a feeling of belonging with others. The process is slow but achievable. It is not easy, but neither is it complicated. And there really is no choice. You must make the commitment to push ahead into the depths of these available relationships.

Belonging to others happens by engaging in shared activities over time. There's nothing secret or complicated about it, no magic tricks—and no shortcuts. Belonging requires time and commitment from you; you've got to be in it for the long haul. The hardest part is finding a starting point. Join an organization and engage the people. Get involved in a church, synagogue, mosque, or other faith community and weave yourself into the lives and loves of the people there. Get over yourself and your fatigue, and open your home to activities and visits. Your fatigue will evaporate with relational activities. Making a quilt is often monotonous and tedious. So is the process of threading your life into the lives of others. But this is how you get to feel like you belong. And this is central to rebuilding your lost refrigerator rights relationships. This is your goal.

Tolerating and Managing Conflict

We have already established that we prize our personal liberty, including the freedom to associate with those with whom we feel comfortable and compatible. If we meet a person and hit it off, we choose to become friends. If, on the other hand, we don't really find it easy to be together, we have the liberty to disassociate, to avoid contact.

You don't have this luxury with family. If you think about it, you're probably related to at least one or two people you wouldn't be caught dead with if you weren't relatives. Even when the love is real and strong, in every family there is interpersonal conflict. Conflict with those you love and care about is part of the fabric of your existence.

Not every family has bitter fights, although almost all have times of intense friction. Every family tolerates a level of conflict on an ongoing basis. None of us is easy to live with, after all. Mercifully, our family puts up with our quirks, habits, and emotional tides. We learn not only to tolerate each other's idiosyncrasies; we eventually come to know how to love each other, even when the other is in one of *those* moods. Sally and I have become accustomed to each other's moods and know how and when to leave each other alone.

My brothers Stephen, Donald, and I have learned over the years to avoid confrontation and conflict. We know each other so well that we avoid trampling on each other's areas of vulnerability. It's one of the ways in which family teaches us; we learn that we have the power to hurt the people we're close to, and (hopefully) we learn the discipline to refrain from causing unnecessary pain. All families do this. We learn to avoid conflict by holding our tongue, by compromising even when it's difficult, and by putting someone else's needs before our own.

The reason we tolerate conflict is that we have made a choice, even if it isn't a conscious choice, to value the relationship above our own self-interest and our need to dominate and control. In the midst of disharmony and antagonism, we regularly make decisions to stay, to keep at it. We do this in spite of strong temptation to just walk out and be at peace. Our love is strong enough to keep us engaged with individuals with whom we are not necessarily compatible. Every family knows that it must keep a lid on certain matters of potential volatility. Learning to tolerate and manage the inevitability of interpersonal tension is central to developing refrigerator rights relationships. Keeping others at arm's length emotionally may help minimize antagonism, but it also guarantees that you will never become close. Allowing and then managing conflict is essential to creating the family you need and crave.

Facilitating Personal Growth and Change

For most of my adult life, I have been attending to my own personal growth and change. I have wanted to become more than just a "better person" as the bland cliché goes. I have been motivated to become a more effective person, personally and professionally. I have spent many years in graduate school and church, pursuing the expansion of my heart, mind, soul, and career opportunities. I have been intent on making my marriage work better, as well as my various roles as stepparent, grandfather, and friend, not to mention minister and counselor. Personal growth and change is the headline of my life.

You may not give a hoot about personal growth. You may never have given it one second's conscious thought. But there is no doubt that your success or failure in life is, in part, related to your ability to adapt and change. Even if you're unaware of it, you *do* change in response to what fate and circumstances have handed to you. Maybe you have faced chronic illness or the death of someone you care about. Maybe you've been stunned by a career reversal. Such predicaments befall each of us periodically, and they mark us forever. We either grow or resist emotional growth when confronted by these external circumstances. We change as a result of our interpretations and reactions to the events of our personal life. For human beings, this means principally our interactions with others. The distinction is not always clear between navel-gazing and genuinely working on the self so as to become more relational—more loving.

At a practical level, the most powerful impetus for personal change and growth happens within the context of our relationships, especially in our emotionally close attachments. Most of us have experienced this firsthand. If you have children, for example, you know that having a baby launches you at high-speed into profound personal change. Think about your life the year before your baby was born and the year after the blessed event. Parents, intentionally or not, eventually submit to the inevitability of a changed life and perspective. It can be an intensely stressful period, but the rewards are tremendous. Then as children grow and become more independent, parents and family engage in a dynamic process of ever-changing relationship. We are forever redefining who we are becoming, from infancy through school days, to graduation and marriage.

Each and every life is fluid and demands constant small shifts and compromises. We watch each other grow and grow older. We celebrate and accommodate, we adjust, and we mourn all the inevitable changes each of us experiences. All the while, our context for growth is people. The healthiest context is family—or any group who become family for us. The best way for us to weather personal change and use it to grow is to be surrounded by those with whom we share refrigerator rights.

This theme of human connection as the soil for personal growth and change is frequently depicted in popular culture. In the odd film *A.I.* (first envisioned by Stanley Kubrick and, after his death, brought to the screen by Steven Spielberg), a mother mourns the death of her young son. She is given a substitute relationship with a robot that looks, acts, and feels like a real boy. She utters the magic programming words, and the robot becomes alive with a love and dedication that mimics reality. The movie depicts the intensity of our need to love and connect as a prerequisite for health and growth. The mother's need to connect with a son figure was so strong that she embraced a relationship with a robot—reluctantly at first, but intensely as the film moved along.

But the public reaction to *A.I.* seems to provide an answer to the very question the film was trying to explore. By the film's end, all but a trace of human existence is gone. The only remaining characters are robots. By all reports, audience reaction to the film was confused and ambivalent. Critical and popular response repeatedly remarked about the cold, uncomfortable feeling toward the robotic characters. Perhaps this reaction shines light on our disconnection and our emerging attachment to the machines that increasingly mediate our reality. Might the film's disappointing box-office performance reflect our sense of isolation from real people and our growing reliance on our appliances and gadgets? We need to connect to real human beings to grow and to change in healthy ways.

A Caveat

Many of you have been involved in unhealthy relationships with unhealthy people or you've seen this happen and don't want to go there. Let's be candid. Even as a therapist, I can tell you that, yes, there are an awful lot of nutcases out there, individuals with a bucket full of social and emotional problems who are unable to form a healthy bond. And some of your own personal qualities may unwittingly attract such needy types like honey attracts bees. Although I've been urging you strongly all through this book to find ways to reconnect with people, obviously you need to use your head and trust your instincts. Of course, you don't want to form close personal bonds with a sociopath, violent abuser, or anyone who devalues you. That much is obvious. But you need also to monitor your inadvertent tendencies to gravitate toward those who have serious unresolved emotional problems. Some complicated souls do make wonderful newfound family members despite their *issues*. Others, however, may draw you into a web of draining or even malevolent entanglements. This, often, is what scares people away from building refrigerator rights relationships.

It's a judgment call, and you may need help with your judgment. Haven't you had the experience of establishing a new friendship or romantic attachment only to be hurt and insulted that everyone else you know is registering alarms and worrying about the person's character or integrity? Or maybe you have been on the other side wondering, "Why can't she see what we see—that he's a complete jerk?" Sometimes everybody else is wrong—but I wouldn't bet on it in most cases. If those you know, love, and trust raise a flag about someone new in your life, it's time to reflect on how accurate and trustworthy your own instincts and feelings are as a guide for finding close emotional attachments. I can recall being in a case conference at the clinic and making the other therapists laugh when I said, in evident frustration, "I just want to say to these people (clients), 'Look, it's not rocket science. Look around at the healthy and successful people you know and start doing what they do!'" As simplistic as it might sound, mimicking the healthy instead of always trusting your own inner voice is sometimes sound advice.

The solution to the problem is to take your time and trust either your own good instincts or the perspective of others you know and trust. Get to know others slowly, patiently, and thoroughly. Just like you did with your screwball cousin who became a drug-addled dropout, you have the right to bail out of any relationship. Many of us are well-meaning and compassionate people, and we feel that if we offer love and acceptance, others will offer us love and acceptance back. And this is generally true. But the bottom line is this: Refrigerator rights relationships are intended to mimic the healthiest family relationships—not the toxic ones. They are never pursued out of pity or in the hopes that you can fix someone else.

Seek out healthy people to get closer to, and you will inevitably cultivate your own mental health while you're at it. If you have unresolved emotional stuff of your own, get to work on it. One of the most blessed things about good refrigerator rights relationships is that they nourish the healthiness in all concerned.

The Faith Community: A Fast Track to Refrigerator Rights

In the church that Glenn and I attend, there are dozens of wonderful people. Yes, of course, they are complicated and fallible and annoy those who live with them. In essence, they are normal and healthy. As I look around our church, there are dozens of men and women who are readily available to become loving fathers and mothers. In your synagogue there are sweet and wise grandparents and energetic and needy little nieces and nephews. In a faith gathering, you can find most of the roles that you either left behind or never had but that you need now to build family. Everyone is there.

Oftentimes, people resist participating because they struggle with their experiences and views about religion. As an ordained minister who was simultaneously working as a nightclub comedian, I frequently encountered this resistance. Comics are an iconoclastic group, not generally sympathetic to joining traditional organizations. What I have most often heard them spit out is their distaste for "organized religion." When they would inquire about my work as an ordained minister, I often sensed a defensive suspicion and even veiled hostility about the church. With some exceptions, I rarely pressed theological matters upon them. Instead, I would tell them about the critical value of finding refrigerator rights relationships within a faith community. Privately, I have always been convinced that once these relationships are under way, most people—even those who enter with uncertainty or antagonism to matters of faith—will come to terms with both what they need to believe and what beliefs they need to surrender. Most people who actually become members of a faith-based group—church or a twelve-step program—eventually find their spiritual needs being met in a way that accords with their intellectual and psychological makeup. Sometimes it takes time, but within faith groups, most people eventually do find home.

In the Christian tradition, the church is referred to as a "body" to emphasize the command to function as one, unified voice of love in the world. This is a pretty accurate standard for understanding the healthy family. Participating in a *faith body* can accelerate the opportunities to replace lost connections that will provide you with the possibilities of reestablishing a family. Even if your motivation is to find emotional sustenance rather than theological or philosophical clarity, the relationships that inevitably form in a good religious community will provide you that and more. If your desire is fast relief from your gnawing worries or from the weight of your depression, immersing yourself in issues of faith, hope, and love may be the healthiest supplement to your medication.

In building refrigerator rights relationships, use whatever resources are available to help you begin the process of reattachment.

If nothing else, the healthy faith community expects its members to be welcoming and inviting to the unattached. Are there closed congregations, rotten churches, and unloving synagogues? You bet. But next door, down the street, or a mile away is the *good* community that is waiting for you.

The Power of Presence

Re-creating attachments is not such a self-conscious business, as we have been led to believe. Walking together through time and shared experience with all the people around you—this is what can grow into more than you ever realized. Presence is more significant than utility. The power of the presence of those you love and to whom you belong is more important than anything in particular that they do for you or with you. We are all seeking the power of the presence of close others: family, refrigerator rights relationships.

You already have everything you need to do this. You know your story, your circumstances, and the motley crew that surrounds you. Take a good look at who is there.

It's your life.

I have confidence that you know what to do.

Points to Remember

❖ If you are socially and emotionally isolated, creating a family is Job Number 1 for you. The process needs time, and it needs lots of ordinary life experiences—some of them dramatic but most mundane.

❖ Think of the people you see at least once a week. They might be co-workers, members of your church or club, people you see at the PTA, or neighbors you sometimes chat with when you mow the lawn or come home with the groceries. These people may be the beginning of your refrigerator rights relationships.

❖ A family is a social environment that nurtures commitment and belonging, tolerates and manages conflict, and facilitates personal growth and change.

Endnotes

Chapter 1

Page 12. Today she is a writer and speaker about grief and loss and attests to change and loss of support as the central variables in the stress of grief. Miller, S. (1999). *Mourning and Dancing*. Deerfield Beach, FL: HCI.

Chapter 2

Page 25. The TV program *Sixty Minutes II* featured a story on the terrorist attacks that left the nation reeling. Fager, J. (Executive Producer). (2001, September 26). *Sixty Minutes II*. New York: Columbia Broadcast System.

Page 26. I'm rarely surprised, these days, to hear of a new study documenting an increase in socially maladaptive or unstable behavior and conclusions that associate these larger social problems with interpersonal separation and aloneness.

DeLuca, S., & Rosenbaum, J. E. (December 20, 2000). Are dropout decisions related to safety concerns, social isolation, and teacher disparagement? [On-line]. Available: http://www.law.harvard.edu/groups/civilrights/publications/dropouts/dropout/deluca.html.

Harrell, A. V., & Petersen, G. E. (Eds.). (1992). Drugs, crime and social isolation: Barriers to urban opportunity. Washington, D.C.: Urban Institute Press.

Robbins, T. W., Jones, G. H., & Wilkinson, L. S. (1996). Behavioral and neurochemical effects of early social deprivation in the rat. *Journal of Psychopharmacology,* 10, 39–47.

Page 28. In 1990, it had crept up to 24 percent. Forstall, R. L., & Fitzsimmons, J. D. (1993, April). Metropolitan Growth and Expansion in the 1980s. Paper presented at the Annual Meeting of the Population Association of America, Cincinnati, OH. Available: http://www.census.gov/population/documentation/twps0006.txt.

Page 31. Consider the statistics. Stanley, S. M., & Markman, H. J. (1999). Facts about marital distress and divorce. [On-line]. Available: http://www.prepinc.com.

Page 33. Yet many people who have them are suffering in silence and secrecy. Rocky Mountain Outreach Center. (2002). Facts about anxiety disorders. [On-line]. Available: http://www.stressanxiety.com/stress3.html.

Page 34. One well-known business web site (Entrepreneur.com) recently pointed out that isolation was the main reason for those hovering feelings of anxiety that just won't go away despite the fact that everything seems to be OK on face. Lyden, S. M. (1999, September). Flying solo: Curb isolation anxiety. [On-line]. Available: http://www.entrepreneur.com/Your_Business/YB_SegArticle/0,4621,230665,00.html.

Page 34. Professor Jean Twenge, a psychologist at Case Western Reserve University recently reported the results of her comprehensive review of studies on over 50,000 people. Twenge J. M. (2000). The age of anxiety? Birth cohort change in anxiety and neuroticism,

1952–1993. *Journal of Personality and Social Psychology,* 79, 1007–1021.

Page 34. The studies focused on trends that have emerged in our culture from the 1950s through the 1990s. Schrof, J. M., and S. Schultz. (1999, March 8). "Melancholy nation." *U.S. News & World Report,* 56–63.

Page 35. They're hyperactive, they get into fights, use drugs and alcohol, break rules, and get into trouble. Schrof, J. M., and S. Schultz. (1999, March 8). "Melancholy nation." *U.S. News & World Report,* 56–63.

Page 35. In America, one suicide takes place about every 17 minutes; suicide now ranks 9th as the cause of death among all people. McIntosh, J. L. (1998). Suicide statistics. [On-line]. Available: http://www.suicidology.org/suicide_statistics.htm

Page 38. Incivilities such as these are becoming the norm as the ranks of the etiquette-challenged grow, warns a business professor who has spent the past four years studying on-the-job behavior. Waggoner, M. (1998, May 30). Workplace incivility costs companies money, study shows. [On-line]. Available: http://www.reporternews.com/biz/civil0530.html.

Page 39. The *Chicago Tribune* offered some facts to consider. U.S. highway deaths rise, experts blame "road rage." (1997, July 18). *Chicago Tribune,* Section 1, p.7.

Page 43. As Harvard researcher Robert Putnam has documented in his painstaking study of American Life, *Bowling Alone,* 10 percent more Americans may be bowling today than in years past, but there are 40 percent fewer people in bowling leagues. Putnam, R. D. (2000). *Bowling Alone: The collapse and revival of American community.* New York: Simon & Schuster.

Chapter 3

Page 48. Data from the U.S. Census Bureau confirmed these suspicions. A staggering number of Americans move each year. Schachter, J. (2001, May). Geographical mobility: March 1999 to March 2000: Current population reports. U.S. Census Bureau, Washington, DC. [On-line]. Available: http://www.census.gov/population/www/socdemo/migrate.html.

Page 55. During one period, from 1993 through 1997, the number of minorities asked to transfer tripled while it remained relatively stable for other groups. Runzheimer International. (1999). Runzheimer reports on relocation: Annual transferee demographic survey. [On-line]. Available: www.jobrelocation.com/runz3.htm.

Page 55. Recently, there has emerged a growing consensus that frequent moves or recent moves may be damaging to child's well-being at least in the short term. DeWit, D. J. (1998). Frequent childhood geographic relocation: Its impact on drug use initiation and the development of alcohol and other drug-related problems among adolescents and young adults. *Addictive Behaviors*, 23, 623–634.

Pages 55–56. An article by a researcher at the U.S. Census Bureau notes that, "Americans in general have high rates of residential mobility, but American children are especially mobile compared to children in several other Western countries and Japan." U.S. Census Bureau (2002). [On-line]. Available: http://www.census.gov.

Page 56. One-fourth of the moves in a person's life occur during childhood. Cornille, T. A. (1993). Support systems and the relocation process for children and families. *Marriage and Family Review*, 19, 281–298.

Page 56. According to a recent Canadian study, 40% of the parents surveyed indicated that their preschool children had moved twice during their lifetime. Kohen, D. E., Hertzman, C., & Wiens, M. (1998). Environmental change and children's competencies. Report W-98-25E on the National Longitudinal Survey of Children and Youth, Human Resources and Development Canada. [On-line]. Available: http://www.hrdc-drhc.gc.ca/arb/publications/research/abw-98-25e.shtml.

Page 62. In their book, *Contemporary Social Problems,* three sociologists recently noted that Americans today experience twice as many transitions as in the recent past. Parrillo, V. N., Stimson, J., & Stimson, A. (1998). Contemporary social problems. Boston: Allyn and Bacon.

Chapter 4

Page 71. Today, the percentage has increased to nearly 25 percent—a five-fold jump. U.S. Census Bureau. (2002). [On-line]. Available: http://www.census.gov.

Chapter 5

Page 83. The content or message of any particular medium has about as much importance as the stenciling on the casing of an atomic bomb. *Playboy* interview (1969, March). Media analyst Marshall McLuhan was among the most provocative and prescient thinkers on the effects of mass media over the last half century. 53–54, 56, 59–62, 64–66, 68, 70, 72, 74, 158.

Page 84. By 1960 that figure had jumped to 90 percent. Liebert, R. M., Sprafkin, J. N., & Davidson, E. S. (1982). *The Early Window: Effects of Television on Children and Youth.* New York: Pergamon Press.

Page 85. Recent surveys document the phenomenal penetration that TV has in our daily lives. Media Awareness Network. (1999). QuickFacts: Media usage: Television. [On-line]. Available: http://www.media-awareness.ca/eng/issues/stats/usetv.htm.

Page 86. These studies dealt with the content of movies (primarily romance and sexuality) and how movies affected children's learning, attitudes, and moral values—even how children slept at night.

Dale, E. (1935). *The Content of Motion Pictures.* New York: Macmillan.

Holaday, P. W., & Stoddard, G.D. (1933). *Getting Ideas from the Movies.* New York: Macmillan.

Peterson, R. C., & Thurstone, L. L. (1933). *Motion Pictures and the Social Attitudes of Children.* New York: Macmillan.

Peters, C. C. (1933). *Motion Pictures and Standards of Morality.* New York: Macmillan.

Dysinger, W. S., & Ruckmick, C. A. (1933). *The Emotional Responses of Children to the Motion Picture Situation.* New York: Macmillan.

Page 86. The Payne Fund Studies were followed up by sporadic investigations of the effects of comic books and radio drama. Wertham, F. (1954). *Seduction of the Innocent.* New York: Rinehart.

Page 87. After over 40 years of scientific research on media effects, there is now a strong consensus that violence, sex, and horror, definitely exert an influence on viewers.

Zillmann, D., Bryant, J., & Huston, A. C. (1994). *Media, Children, and the Family: Social Scientific, Psychodynamic, and Clinical Perspectives.* Hillsdale, NJ: Lawrence Erlbaum.

Bryant, J., & Zillmann, D. (2002). *Media Effects: Advances in Theory and Research.* Hillsdale, NJ: Lawrence Earbaum.

Pages 87–88. This means that roughly 90 percent of the aggression or lack of aggression has to be explained by other factors. Sparks, G. G. (2001). *Media Effects: A Basic Overview.* San Francisco, CA: Wadsworth.

Page 89. Brandon Centerwall, a University of Washington researcher, presented an exhaustive analysis that showed that the homicide rate in the United States doubled after the introduction of television. Centerwall, B. S. (1989). Exposure to television as a cause of violence. In G. Comstock, (Ed.), Public communication and behavior: Vol. 2, (pp. 1–58). San Diego: Academic Press.

Page 90. Like the high school killers in Littleton, Colo., Smith went after anyone who believed—in God, in family, in the rightness of their own existence, and anyone who belonged. Dobie, K. (1999, July 19). The unbearable whiteness of being. Salon News, 1–3. [On-line]. Available: http://www.salon.com/news/feature/1999/07/19/white/index.html.

Page 90. There may be more me, less we. Scheuer, J. (1999). The sound bite society: Television and the American mind. New York: Four Walls and Eight Windows.

Page 90. Internet researchers have already warned us about the possibility that over-reliance on this new medium produces greater social isolation. Kraut, R., Patterson, M., Lundmark, V., Kiesler, S., Mukopadhyay, T., & Scherlis, W. (1998). Internet paradox: A social technology that reduces social involvement and psychological well-being. *American Psychologist,* 53, 1017–1031.

Page 92. They can analyze and articulate the attitudes they believe the characters will express in various circumstances. Perse, E. M., & Rubin, R. B. (1989). Attribution in social and parasocial relationships. *Communication Research,* 16, 59–77.

Page 94. Over a decade ago, two communication researchers recognized that talk radio was functioning, not so much as *mass* communication, but as *interpersonal* communication. Armstrong, C. B., & Rubin, A. M. (1989). Talk radio as interpersonal communication. *Journal of Communication, 39,* 84–94.

Page 94. In an article entitled, "Talk Radio: The Private-Public Catharsis," the author noted that both callers and listeners in the talk-radio audience apparently have their needs for interpersonal communication partially met by the experience of the radio talk show. Avery, R. K. (1990). Talk radio: The private-public catharsis. In G. Gumpert & S. L. Fish (Eds.), Talking to strangers: Mediated therapeutic communication (pp. 87–97). Norwood, NJ: Ablex Publishing.

Page 95. Audience members might react to media performers and the characters they portray as if the performers were actual friends. Dominick, J. (1996). *The Dynamics of Mass Communication.* New York: McGraw-Hill.

Page 96. According to the most recent data, nearly 9 percent of the world's population is online now. ComputerScope, Ltd. (2001). How many online? [On-line]. Available: http://www.nua.ie/surveys/how_many_online/world.html.

Page 97. In one recent survey, researchers at Carnegie Mellon University studied the impact of communicating over the Internet on emotional health. Kraut, R., Patterson, M., Lundmark, V., Kiesler, S., Mukopadhyay, T., & Scherlis, W. (1998). Internet paradox: A social technology that reduces social involvement and psychological well-being. *American Psychologist, 53,* 1017–1031.

Page 99. "Generally, strong personal ties are supported by physical proximity." Kraut, R., Patterson, M., Lundmark, V., Kiesler, S.,

Mukopadhyay, T., & Scherlis, W. (1998). Internet paradox: A social technology that reduces social involvement and psychological well-being. *American Psychologist,* 53, 1017–1031.

Page 101. Media are full participants in our social and natural world. Reeves, B., & Nass, C. (1996). The media equation: How people treat computers, television, and new media like real people and places. Cambridge: Cambridge University Press.

Chapter 6

Page 108. Psychologists call this the "illusion of personal invulnerability." Zimbardo, P. G., Ebbesen, E. B. & Maslach, C. (1977). Influencing attitudes and changing behavior. Reading, MA: Addison-Wesley.

Page 113. They need good friends. Lefcourt, H. M., Martin, R. A., & Saleh, W. E. (1984). Locus of control and social support: Interactive moderators of stress. *Journal of Personality and Social Psychology,* 47, 378–389.

Page 117. Marsha Richins has argued that consumer desire definitely shapes the entire marketing and advertising industry. Richins, M. L., & Dawson, S. (1992). A consumer values orientation for materialism and its measurement: Scale development and validation. *Journal of Consumer Research,* 19, 303–316.

Page 118. In an article that appeared in *Social Indicators Research,* Joseph Sirgy found that whether or not a person is satisfied with their present standard of living is a critical ingredient in determining their quality of life. Sirgy, J. (1998). Materialism and quality of life. *Social Indicators Research,* 43, 227–260.

Page 118. Two researchers found that students who were highly materialistic also tended to score higher on measures of envy and social anxiety than students who were less focused on possessions. Schroeder, J. E., & Dugal, S. S. (1995). Psychological correlates of the materialism construct. *Journal of Social Behavior & Personality,* 10, 243–253.

Page 118. A recent study found that young people who suffer from disrupted families adopt more materialistic attitudes than do young people who are raised in intact families. Rindfleisch, A., Burroughs, J. E., & Denton, F. (1997). Family structure, materialism, and compulsive consumption. *Journal of Consumer Research,* 23, 312–325.

Page 119. Another group of scholars observed that young people who experience feelings of insecurity that result from family disruption may attempt to assuage their insecurities by seeking control over objects or people. An, C., Haveman, R., & Wolfe, B. (1993). Teen out-of-wedlock births and welfare receipt: The role of childhood events and economic circumstances. *Review of Economics and Statistics,* 75, 195–208.

Page 119. Our findings provide considerable evidence that family structure is related to both materialism and compulsive consumption. Rindfleisch, A., Burroughs, J. E., & Denton, F. (1997). Family structure, materialism, and compulsive consumption. *Journal of Consumer Research,* 23, 312–325.

Page 119. The authors of this study went on to note that "physical objects and acts of consumption can serve as important replacements for human contact." Rindfleisch, A., Burroughs, J. E., & Denton, F. (1997). Family structure, materialism, and compulsive consumption. *Journal of Consumer Research,* 23, 312–325.

Page 121. Psychologist David Johnson argues that we depend on human relationships like these to provide, "the essential competencies required to survive in our world, and for fun, excitement, comfort, love, personal confirmation, and fulfillment." Johnson, D. W. (1997). Reaching out: Interpersonal effectiveness and self-actualization. Boston, MA.: Allyn and Bacon.

Page 124. John Robinson's recent book, *Time for Life: The Surprising Ways Americans Use Their Time,* reports that Americans, "have almost five hours of free time more a week than they did in the 1960s." Robinson, J. P., & Godbey, G. (1997). Time for life: The surprising ways Americans use their time. University Park, PA: Pennsylvania State University Press.

Page 124. One college president was so impressed with the problems of the stress-filled, fast-paced life in America that he decided to write an entire book urging people to adopt, "the simple life." Shi, D. E. (1985). The simple life: Plain living and high thinking in American culture. New York: Oxford University Press.

Chapter 7

Page 130. Nouwen, Henri (1997). *Bread or the Journey.* San Francisco, CA: HarperCollins.

Page 135. In comparative studies on levels of job stress and worker dissatisfaction, the data show that the people of individualistic cultures typically report much higher stress levels than do the people of collectivist cultures. Chiu, R. K., & Kosinski, F. A., Jr. (1999). The role of affective dispositions in job satisfaction and work strain. Comparing collectivist and individualist societies. *International Journal of Psychology,* 34, 19–28.

Page 136. Close family members provide real emotional support. Coombs, R. H., & Fawzy, F. I. (1982). The effect of martial status on stress in medical school. *American Journal of Psychiatry,* 139, 1490–1493.

Page 139. Berkman concluded that, "Here we have a risk factor related to emotional support that's in the magnitude of the strongest cardiovascular risk factors that we know of." Harvard School of Public Health. (1997). Gateway to world health: Social and individual aspects of longevity. [On-line]. Available: http://www.hsph. harvard.edu/digest/social.html.

Page 142. David Myers, an authority on close relationships, has documented the findings of several major studies on the relationship between health and our connection to other people. Myers, D. G. (1999). Close relationships and quality of life. In D. Kahneman & E. Diener (Eds.). Well-being: The foundations of hedonic psychology (pp. 374–391). New York, NY: Russell Sage.

Page 142. The results clearly showed that after going through these highly stressful events, people were much more susceptible to disease. Dohrenwend, B., Pearlin, L., Clayton, P., Hamburg, B., Dohrenwend, B. P., Riley, M., and Rose, R. (1982). Report on stress and life events. In G. R. Elliott and C. Eisdorfer (Eds.), Stress and human health: Analysis and implications of research (pp. 55–80). New York: Springer-Verlag.

Page 142. Death among the widowed population was twice as likely in the week following their partner's death than it was for the non-widowed population. Kaprio, J., Koskenvuo, M., and Rita, H. (1987). Mortality after bereavement: A prospective study of 95,647 widowed persons. *American Journal of Public Health,* 77, 283–287.

Page 143. Even in a disease as serious as leukemia, one study shows that social support from family and friends over a two-year period resulted in a 54 percent survival rate, compared to only 20 percent when social support just wasn't there. Colon, E. A., Callies, A. L., Popkin, M. K., and McGlave, P. B. (1991). Depressed mood and other variables related to bone marrow transplantation survival in acute leukemia. Psychosomatics, 32, 420–25.

Page 143. A number of other studies show the same effect also occurs in patients who have suffered heart attacks.

Case, R. B., Moss, A. J., Case, N., McDermott, M., and Eberly, S. (1992). "Living alone after myocardial infarction: Impact on prognosis." *Journal of the American Medical Association,* 267, 515–19.

Williams, R. B., Barefoot, J. C., Califf, R. M., Haney, T. L., Saunders, W. B., Pryor, D. B., Hlatky, M. A., Siegler, I. C., and Mark, D. B. (1992). "Prognostic importance of social and economic resources among medically treated patients with angiographically documented coronary artery disease." *Journal of the American Medical Association,* 267, 520–24.

Chapter 8

Page 162. While adolescents appear to be at a higher level of risk, some children actually seem to thrive after their parents split. Hetherington, E.M., & Kelly, J. (2000). *For Better or for Worse: Divorce Reconsidered.* New York: W. W. Norton.

About the Authors

Dr. Will Miller holds a Master's and Doctorate in Urban Education from the University of Massachusetts, a Master's in Clinical Social Work from Columbia University, and Master's of Divinity from the Union Theological Seminary in New York. He is a therapist with training in psychoanalysis, family counseling, and a specialty in the treatment of addictions, and was spokesperson for the National Institute on Mental Health's Campaign on Depression Awareness. Dr. Miller is also an ordained minister who is the Pastor of Teaching and Counseling at University Church at Purdue University. In addition, Will is currently in great demand as one of the country's top public speakers for corporations and other organizations. He performed stand-up comedy for fifteen years, headlining comedy clubs and working as an opening act for many celebrities. Will was the host of the NBC daytime talk show *The Other Side,* about the paranormal and unexplained phenomena. He is perhaps best known since 1992 as an on-air spokesman for Nick-at-Nite on the Nickelodeon cable network. In his "Why We Watch" spots, he has analyzed the hidden psychological meaning of classic TV programs. His book *Why We Watch: Killing the Gilligan Within,* is a satire that humorously outlines the new "self-help" therapeutic technique he calls "Teletherapy." He lives with his wife, author and grief expert, Dr. Sally Downham Miller, in West Lafayette, Indiana, and in New York City.

Dr. Glenn Sparks is a professor of Mass Communication at Purdue University. He holds a Master's in Communication from Northern Illinois University and a Doctorate in Communication Arts from the University of Wisconsin–Madison. In addition to his present position at Purdue, he has held faculty appointments at Cleveland State University and Wheaton College. He is recognized as one of the nation's leaders in the study of media effects, especially in the area of media that frighten children. Recently he has conducted groundbreaking research on the effects of media that depict paranormal themes. With more than fifty scholarly publications to his credit, alongside twenty years of teaching, Professor Sparks offers an important voice in the current struggle to understand what living in a media-saturated culture is doing to us all. Glenn Sparks lives with his wife, social psychologist Dr. Cheri Sparks, in West Lafayette, Indiana.